The
Cooperative
Society

Praise for the First Edition of
The Cooperative Society

"*The Cooperative Society* . . . does an outstanding job of explaining the context for change and, just as importantly, the urgent need for such a change."

Charles Gould, past Director-General, International Co-operative Alliance

"*The Cooperative Society* is a refreshing and hopeful analysis of major trends in human behavior."

Judy Ziewacz, former President and CEO, National Cooperative Business Association/CLUSA

"I liked *The Cooperative Society* a lot. It's both forward-looking and grand in its historical context – and irredeemably hopeful, especially given the current political craziness."

Burt Solomon, contributing editor, *The Atlantic* and *National Journal*

"*The Cooperative Society* is a hopeful and practical blueprint of where we all need to place our focus if we wish to contribute to the evolution of a more resilient, egalitarian, peaceful and co-operative society. With wonderfully informative graphics, [the authors] present encouraging insights on just how far we have come already, and where we need to put our efforts now to get us to the next stage of human history."

Wendy Holm, agronomist, columnist, journalist, writer,
Bowen Island, British Columbia, Canada

"*The Cooperative Society* lays out major drivers of our socio/political/economic environment, but it also develops a useful framework for measuring and monitoring these factors over time."

Walden Swanson, founder and Director Emeritus, CoMetrics

"This is the ultimate message of this book: We as a species are not destined to destroy ourselves and our planet. We can make the transition from a destructive society to a cooperative one. And we can make major progress on that transition between now and 2030."

From the Conclusion

The Cooperative Society

The Next Stage of Human History
Second Edition

E.G. Nadeau, Ph.D., & Luc Nadeau, M.S.
Graphics by Luc Nadeau

ISBN 978-0-9980662-3-3
Both editions of *The Cooperative Society* are available as an eBook.

The cover image is from the Cueva de las Manos—Cave of the Hands,
Santa Cruz, Argentina, "123 Royalty Free" https://www.123rf.com
The hand silhouettes are estimated to be over 9,000 years old. They symbolize
to the authors the cooperative efforts of the artists and the temporal, spatial,
and spiritual links that connect the members of the human species.

Design by Smiling Dog Design

Printed and bound in the United States of America
Second Edition; first printing October 2018

Published by E.G. Nadeau, Ph.D., and Luc Nadeau, M.S.
1. Economic history and conditions
2. Social history and conditions
3. Social problems
4. Social reform

eg@thecooperativesociety.org
www.thecooperativesociety.org

Dedication

This book is dedicated to Kofi Annan, who played
a pivotal role in the formation and implementation
of the Millennium Development Goals program
when he was Secretary General of the United Nations.

Table of Contents

Section C: Taking action

Section D: Conclusion

Section E: Appendices

Foreword

This tightly organized book will make you think and will give you reason to hope.

The viewpoint is long. The authors, E.G. Nadeau and Luc Nadeau, assess the pathway of humans on Earth over the past several hundred thousand years, and the potential of humans going forward.

They identify major eras of economic development – hunting and gathering, simple agriculture, and large organizations providing most every type of product and service. They boldly suggest that the next era will be the cooperative society, wherein people work together locally, at smaller scale, with greater democratic participation, generating less inequality, with reduced environmental degradation. Indeed, the authors suggest that the transition to the cooperative society has already begun.

To be sure, anyone can make a statement about what the future will be like. But the authors have deep experience in cooperative organization, and they base their projection in large-scale data trends. This strategy of predicting the future does several things well: it gets our attention, it illuminates their reasoning, and it provides markers for assessing whether they will be right, or not so right. Thus, they are not merely advocating a set of values, but also taking intellectual responsibility for the assessment. This is a highly desirable combination of reasoning, innovation, and testing, which are hallmarks of the best-applied social science.

The authors of *The Cooperative Society* offer seven measures representing economic, political, social, and environmental transition to the cooperative society: (1) concentration of economic power, (2) wealth and income equality, (3) deaths from domestic and international conflicts, (4) more or fewer people living in democratic countries, (5) population change, (6) improving or deteriorating quality of life, and (7) improving or deteriorating environmental conditions.

By any standard, this is an ambitious list. Again, this is responsible social science. In a word, they are willing to be proven wrong.

One can imagine a set of systematic tests for these outcomes that does not require full data on the progress of human history—especially systematic testing of cooperative innovations, with appropriate comparisons or controls. Such tests would be challenging enough to undertake, but not impossible. If the authors turn out to be correct, such tests would be a great investment. Ideally, this book and following discussions will lead to more applied research taking up this agenda.

Placing *The Cooperative Society* in a larger discussion, I am reminded of the work of Steven Pinker, most recently in the book *Enlightenment NOW* (2018). Pinker is similarly optimistic about the human future, and his analytic strategy is also data-based. He sees the potential for massive progress based on reason and humanism – the touchstones of the Enlightenment.

E.G. Nadeau and Luc Nadeau certainly embrace values of the Enlightenment, but emphasize as well the importance of cooperative organization as a promising pathway to future human progress. This is a more specific agenda than Pinker's, growing from their experience with cooperative organization. The authors outline key areas of work, and envision opportunities for changes that can be made by 2030, which is the target date for both the Paris Accord on Climate Change and the United Nation's Sustainable Development Goals.

Overall, the great contribution of *The Cooperative Society* is that it has implications for action and research, and the authors put these implications on the table.

Michael Sherraden, Ph.D.
George Warren Brown Distinguished University Professor
Washington University, St. Louis, Missouri
September 2018

Reference: Pinker, S. (2018). *Enlightenment NOW: The case for reason, science, humanism, and progress.* New York: Viking.

Preface

Are we on the verge of a new stage of human history – one characterized by cooperation and equitable access to resources rather than by conflict and extreme inequality?

The authors posed this question in the first edition of *The Cooperative Society: The Next Stage of Human History*, published in September 2016. We selected seven broad measures of economic, political, social, and environmental change in order to gauge progress. We discovered that in some ways, we are moving in a more cooperative and equitable direction. In other ways, we aren't.

Since our goal is to make such a transformation more likely, we will revise and publish *The Cooperative Society: The Next Stage of Human History* with new observations periodically through 2030. The 2018 edition, which evaluates progress and recommends ways we can take positive action, is available as a book and a PDF file.

The book is intended to be read by a broad range of people, especially those who are interested in the state of the world today, where things may be headed in the near future, and what we can do to improve conditions for our species and the planet. In particular, the audience for the book includes:

- People who are active in cooperatives, mutual insurance companies, social enterprises, and other not-for-profit organizations

- Progressive elected officials and government employees at all levels

- Socially responsible business leaders and employees

- Citizens who are active in their communities

- Faculty and students at secondary schools, colleges, and universities

Readers can learn more about The Cooperative Society Project via our website and our bimonthly newsletter. We offer other publications and videos, make presentations, and give interviews as well. We hope that you will join us on this journey of exploration and social action by sharing information with others, taking action in your local communities, and contributing your ideas and suggestions to: eg@thecooperativesociety.org

Acknowledgments

We would like to thank the following people for their advice, professional expertise, and support of *The Cooperative Society* for the first and/or second editions of our book: Isaac Nadeau, Jim Arts, Christina Clamp, Charles Gould, Dave Grace, Wendy Holm, Jerry Huffman, Dan Nordley, David Riemer, Gianluca Salvatori, Carrie Scherpelz, Michael Sherraden, Burt Solomon, Jill Stevenson, Walden Swanson, David Thompson, Tom Webb, Judy Ziewacz, and others.

Our thanks to Patricia Miller, editor of the first edition, and Sue Filbin, editor of the second edition and designer of both books.

Needless to say, the authors take responsibility for this book's content, including any errors it may contain.

Introduction

As we wrote in the first edition of *The Cooperative Society: The Next Stage of Human History*, we humans may be moving beyond our conflict-filled past toward a society in which cooperation is the predominant way we relate to one another and to our planet.

Why do we believe such a societal transformation may be taking place at this point in our history? One key factor may be that humans no longer feel compelled to fight over scarce resources because we now have the means, organizational skills, and technology to meet everyone's basic needs.

In this book, we expand on the hypothesis that humans may be on the threshold of a new historical stage, one characterized by cooperation, democracy, the equitable distribution of resources, and a sustainable relationship with nature.

The Cooperative Society is organized in three parts: A description of the hypothesis, research on the hypothesis based on measurement of seven broad sets of variables, and a presentation of recommendations for moving toward a more cooperative society.

In addition to the broad update of information, analyses, and recommendations, this second edition also:

- Consolidates the analyses of cooperatives and for-profit businesses into one broader chapter on the direction of the world economy. This new chapter also presents information on "social enterprises"

– businesses that put service before profits -- and on "socially responsible" activities by for-profit businesses

- Adds "population change" as a seventh measurement category related to the cooperative transition

- Revises the recommendations in Section C to place a greater emphasis on actions that people can take as individuals and at the community level

While we objectively report and analyze the scientific data for and against the transition to a more cooperative society, we are also advocates. *The Cooperative Society* is a call to action, not simply the testing of a hypothesis. We, as humans, have the ability to shape our society. Our purpose is to motivate and assist readers in restructuring our economic, political, and social behavior – and our institutions in ways that are better for humanity and for our planet. We believe that a cooperative transition would be a momentous, positive step forward for our species.

Section A:
The Cooperative Society hypothesis

The Cooperative Society
hypothesis

The cooperative society is a potential new stage of human history, characterized by economic and political democracy, cooperative international relations, and a symbiotic relationship with nature. The cooperative society would replace our current stage of history, which is characterized by a small number of large countries and for-profit corporations that dominate the world economy; a mix of authoritarian and democratic governments; a low quality of life for many of us; conflict-based interaction within and among nations; and a destructive relationship with the environment.

We may already have begun the transition to the cooperative society in the latter half of the 20th century and the beginning of the 21st. If such a transition is occurring:

- This emerging society would be a major paradigm shift, on a scale that has happened only a few times since we evolved as a species about 300,000 years ago.[1]

- For the first time in over 5,000 years,[2] we would have a society that is not dominated by religious, military, political, and/or economic elites.

- Instead, our society would be based on cooperation and democracy rather than conflict, control by the few, and extreme inequality.

The Cooperative Society examines the premise that humans are on the threshold of such a momentous historical change, making possible the realization of our most broadly and deeply held social values.[3]

This book sketches the major stages of human history to date; outlines the key ways in which a cooperative society would differ from these prior stages; defines, analyzes, and scores seven measures related to the cooperative transition; and recommends ways for us to make this transition.

This book is part of a long-term effort to define and measure movement toward or away from the cooperative society. A major goal is to present a set of evolving recommendations to help us make the cooperative transition a reality.

Stages of human history

There are many ways to characterize the history of Homo sapiens – technology (Stone Age, Bronze Age, Iron Age, etc.); social organization (migratory bands, villages, cities, etc.); economic activities; or a combination of traits.

We will emphasize the perspective of economic activities. In this approach, the major stages of human history can be classified as: hunting and gathering, simple agriculture, and an age of increasingly complex and diversified economic activity.

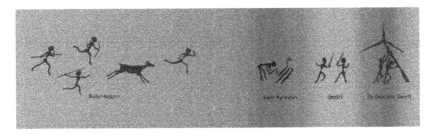

For over 90% of our history, we humans relied on **hunting and gathering** as our means of survival.[4] Through both archaeology and by examining the behavior of isolated groups of hunter-gatherers and other primates today, we can conclude that these ancestors lived in relatively small groups – usually 30 to 100 people; they were fairly egalitarian in social behavior and distribution of resources; they had mixed levels of conflict; and their relationship with nature was primarily symbiotic.[5]

Simple agriculture began in a number of locations between 10,000 and 15,000 years ago. Some scientists have concluded that the primary reason for the emergence of agriculture was increasing population density and the concurrent limitations on a hunting and gathering lifestyle. Farming permitted higher concentrations of people, required a less nomadic way of life, and led to the establishment of permanent or semi-permanent villages.

With more humans living close to one another, many scientists believe that society became more hierarchical, although not dramatically so. Because of fixed villages, the potential for conflict with other agricultural groups and nomadic bands also increased. The small number of humans and the limited scale of agricultural production meant that negative impacts on the environment were usually minor.[6]

The age of **increasingly diversified economic activity** can be roughly estimated as beginning about 5,000 years ago with the emergence of larger concentrations of people in and around cities. As agricultural techniques improved, farmers produced greater surpluses that could support more non-farming activities. This allowed some members of society to specialize in other types of work or become political, economic, and/or religious elites. Also, with increasing concentrations of people in and near cities, the potential for conflict increased – both within these urban-based settings and between them and other city-states and nomadic groups. As these population centers grew in size, they had a greater negative impact on the environment.[7]

These broad stages of history do not include a separate category for capitalism. We consider capitalism as part of the age of increasingly diversified economic activity. The patterns that characterized the growth of cities a few thousand years ago – the stratification of society, the heightened levels of conflict, and the increasing negative impacts on the environment – can be seen as a continuum leading up to our present "capitalist" world.

In the late 20th and early 21st centuries, we may be on the threshold of a new stage of human history – **the cooperative society.** The transition to this new stage is characterized by a mostly urban population and political and economic power that remains highly concentrated, but also has an increasing level of democracy. Resources are distributed very inequitably, but there are some signs that distribution is improving. Conflict persists within and among many of the world's countries, but the number of deaths resulting from these conflicts is decreasing. Humans continue to degrade the environment, but efforts are increasing to remediate unsustainable practices.

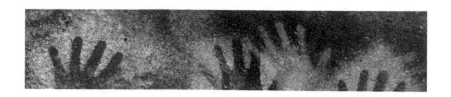

Section B:
Measuring the transition to The Cooperative Society

Measuring the transition to The Cooperative Society

The best way we can think of to begin this section of the book is with this quote from the introduction to the Universal Declaration of Human Rights approved by the members of the United Nations in 1948:

> In perhaps the most resonant and beautiful words of any international agreement, "All human beings are born free and equal in dignity and rights." The commitments made by all States in the Universal Declaration of Human Rights are in themselves a mighty achievement, discrediting the tyranny, discrimination and contempt for human beings that have marked human history.
>
> The Universal Declaration promises to all the economic, social, political, cultural and civic rights that underpin a life free from want and fear. They are not a reward for good behavior. They are not country-specific, or particular to a certain era or social group. They are the inalienable entitlements of all people, at all times, and in all places — people of every color, from every race and ethnic group; whether or not they are disabled; citizens or migrants; no matter their sex, their class, their caste, their creed, their age or sexual orientation.[8]

If we were to ascribe a symbolic beginning of the transition to the cooperative society, it would be the adoption of this Declaration.

During the first half of the 20th century, there were two world wars with a combined total of about 100 million deaths.[9] The Declaration signaled a recognition by the countries of the world that conflict was not an effective way to solve human problems. International cooperation and respect for human life were far better alternatives.

The human and planetary toll of rising world temperatures due primarily to the burning of fossil fuels and deforestation was not yet on the radar screen of the nascent United Nations in 1948. But beginning in 1992, the UN took on the international coordinating role so nations could together combat the negative consequences of increasing greenhouse gases in the atmosphere.

The UN now states that, "Climate change is one of the major challenges of our time and adds considerable stress to our societies and to the environment. From shifting weather patterns that threaten food production, to rising sea levels that increase the risk of catastrophic flooding, the impacts of climate change are global in scope and unprecedented in scale. Without drastic action today, adapting to these impacts in the future will be more difficult and more costly."[10]

Three critical sets of international goals have their origins in the UN Declaration of Human Rights and the UN's commitment to averting climate change disaster:

- The Millennium Development Goals, adopted unanimously by the General Assembly in 2000, in effect from 2000 to 2015[11]

- The Sustainable Development Goals, adopted unanimously in 2015 and to be completed by 2030[12]

- The Paris Agreement, an international commitment to reduce greenhouse gas emissions, signed in 2016.[13] (The only country out of 195 UN members indicating its intent to withdraw from this agreement is the United States under President Donald Trump.)[14]

These three sets of goals signal a commitment to reduce poverty and improve the quality of life and the environment in every country of the world. The Sustainable Development Goals continue and expand on the commitments of the Millennium Development Goals, and also incorporate the aims of the Paris Agreement to "take urgent action to combat climate change and its impacts."[15]

A main objective of this book is to determine how we are doing as a world community in living up to the human rights standards and climate change targets laid out by UN members. Important sources of information for the book are reports by the two development goal programs and the United Nations Framework Convention on Climate Change.[16]

Selecting the measures for analyzing the transition

The authors had the difficult task of selecting representative measures of the transition to a cooperative society. Key selection criteria included:

- Not burying the reader in too many variables or too much complexity

- Avoiding oversimplification or bias in the measures selected

- Including a range of social, economic, political, and environmental measures to create a balanced review of the transition

- Finding worldwide data sets that are updated periodically

Based on these criteria, the authors identified seven primary measures. For some of these measures, several data sets were used – for example, there are two main sources measuring the extent of country-by-country democracy in the world. We did a comparative analysis of these datasets.

Seven measures

Here are the seven measures representing economic, political, social, and environmental components of a transition to the cooperative society:

1. Concentration of economic power

- To what extent is the world's economy dominated by a small percentage of corporations and countries? Is this level of domination increasing or decreasing? Are checks and balances and alternative forms of business being developed and applied to reduce the negative consequences of this concentration?

- Importance of this measure: As long as economic decision-making is dominated by the few, the rest of us are dependent on the choices that they make. This has consequences for fluctuations in the economy (for example The Great Recession), jobs and income, the quality of life, and the quality of the environment.

2. Wealth and income inequality

- Is the distribution of wealth and income becoming more or less unequal among the world's households? Among households within each country?

- Importance of this measure: Concentration of wealth and income has consequences for the economic well-being of the rest of us. We earn less, receive fewer social benefits, and have less influence over political decision-making that affects our day-to-day lives.

3. Deaths from conflict

- Are the number of deaths from international and civil wars increasing or decreasing? Are the number of homicides around the world increasing or decreasing?

- Importance of this measure: The primary issue is the everyday safety of individuals and families. As countries, ethnic and religious groups, and other factions increasingly resolve their differences through negotiation and cooperative agreements, we will all be safer.

4. Democracy

- Is the number of countries with democratic governments rising or falling? Is the percentage of people living in democratic countries increasing or decreasing?

- Importance of this measure: The ability to elect our political leaders and participate in other decision-making that affects our lives is the hallmark of a democratic society.

5. Population change

- What is the rate of worldwide population growth? Is this rate increasing or decreasing?

- Importance of this measure: The more people on the planet, the greater the pressure we put on resource allocation and the quality of the environment. If we can slow the rate of population growth, and eventually reduce it to zero – through non-coercive means – we can more easily improve the quality of life of all humans with less danger of degrading the environment.

6. Quality of life

- Overall, are humans living healthier and more economically secure lives than in the past? Is this trend increasing?

- Importance of this measure: A decent quality of life for all humans is a fundamental international goal embodied in the United Nations Declaration of Human Rights.

7. The environment

- Are human actions worsening or improving the environment? In particular, what is the current status and projected impact of global warming?

- Importance of this measure: The quality of the environment affects the health of humans, other animals, and plants. If we degrade our climate, we harm all life. In particular, the emission of greenhouse gases, primarily caused by humans, could cause major damage to the earth and its inhabitants in the 21st century.

In Chapters 1 through 7 we use these seven measures to determine trends toward or away from a more cooperative society.

Chapter 1

Economic power

"Those who have the gold, rule." So goes a warped definition of the Golden Rule. In a cooperative society, there would not be a small group of businesses, governmental officials, or others who control a hugely disproportionate share of the world's economic power. But in contemporary society – and in fact for the past 5,000 years or so – such a skewed distribution of economic power has been the norm.[17]

The purpose of this chapter is to examine to what extent economic power is concentrated in the world today and whether or not this economic control by the few is increasing or decreasing. These issues are important because small groups of large corporations, governments, and wealthy individuals often make self-serving decisions and sometimes create havoc and destitution for much of the rest of the world's population.

In the 2016 edition of *The Cooperative Society,* we presented data on large publicly traded corporations and on cooperatives and mutual insurance companies. These two types of businesses have radically different goals and values. Publicly traded corporations have as their primary goal generating profits for their investors, board members, and upper management. Co-ops and mutuals are owned and democratically controlled by their individual and organizational members. Their primary goal is to provide goods and services to these members.

Our 2016 analysis determined that economic concentration was very high, and increasing, among publicly traded corporations. At the same time, the data showed significant growth in the early 21st century in the economic power of cooperatives and mutual insurance companies. We concluded that these results presented no clear pattern of structural economic change in the past couple of decades. In some ways, economic decision-making was becoming more concentrated and in other ways more democratic.

We present updated information on these two types of businesses in this chapter to see if any significant change has taken place in the two most recent years for which data are available.

Before we present this information, however, we lay out a more comprehensive context for understanding different business models and their implications for the future of our species and our planet.

Comparing types of businesses

Investor-owned corporations and member-owned co-ops and mutual insurance companies represent only part of the business world. There are two other powerful types of businesses that have a major influence on our lives: corporations with substantial state ownership, and "closely held" (not publicly traded) large corporations. There are data available on both of these business types, but they are not easily quantifiable on a world scale nor measurable over time. Thus, we need to keep in mind the power of these business types and trends related to their growth or decline, even though it is difficult to measure these tendencies systematically.

The analysis of business types is complicated by overlapping corporate structures. For example, four of the largest businesses in the world are state-owned Chinese banks. However, these banks are also publicly traded, even though the largest share of ownership by far is the government of China.[18] Thus, they are state-owned and publicly traded at the same time. But guess who wins the vote on any action considered by the stockholders?

Saudi Aramco is the largest state-owned business in the world as measured by 2017 sales of $455 billion. Aramco is considering a public offering of stock, which at this time is on hold.[19] By the way, the largest company in the world based on sales is Walmart, at about $500 billion.[20]

The largest "closely held" company is Samsung, owned primarily by a South Korean family. In 2017, it had $223 billion in sales. To add a further complication, Samsung is listed in the Forbes Global 2000 as a publicly traded company. Measured by annual sales, it is the 11th-largest business on the Forbes list. Samsung's limited stock holdings allow it to be classified as publicly traded, even though the large majority of its ownership is by a single family.[21]

The other largest closely held businesses are Vitol, a Dutch commodity trading company; Cargill, a US-based company primarily involved in agriculture-related products; Trafigura, headquartered in the Netherlands and specializing in base metals and energy; and Koch Industries, based in the US, focusing on chemical manufacturing, and owned primarily by the infamous, right-wing Koch brothers.[22]

And then there is the largest category of business types: small businesses – small corporations, partnerships, and sole proprietorships. As with businesses that are partially or fully state-owned and with closely held companies, it is very difficult to analyze the number and growth trends of small businesses, especially on a world scale.

There is one more category of business that we would like to highlight in this chapter: social enterprises. These businesses can be simply defined as companies that "put service before profit."[23] Many social enterprises provide services and products related to children, the elderly, people with disabilities, jobseekers, and others. These businesses can also provide a wide range of housing, environmental, development, and other services. Some social enterprises are organized as co-ops. Social enterprises often contract with local governments to provide services. For example, the city of Bologna, Italy, contracts for about 85% of its social services through social enterprise co-ops, including childcare, eldercare, and a wide range of other services.[24]

Social enterprises have become a rapidly growing phenomenon in the past decade, particularly in Western Europe.[25] Since the official recognition of the Italian social cooperative model in 1991, six other European countries – Belgium, France, Ireland, Poland, Slovakia, and Spain – have established statutes for social enterprises. There are approximately 230,000 social enterprises in these six countries with an estimated 1.5 million employees.[26]

The Cooperative Society Project featured an article on social enterprises in its January 2018 newsletter.[27] Measuring the number of these enterprises and their growth over time is difficult. Thus, it will be important to watch their development during the coming decades. For the time being, we will have to do so without good international quantitative data.

Recognizing that there are a number of major types of businesses, we confine our quantitative analysis to two major categories – co-ops/mutuals and publicly traded companies – for several reasons:

- They represent two distinct business models – the primacy of service vs. the primacy of profit

- There is reliable, worldwide longitudinal data for both

- They account for a large percentage of the planet's business activity

1. Cooperatives
2016 data
Cooperative businesses are owned and democratically controlled by their members. (We included mutually

owned businesses and credit unions within this definition of cooperatives.) Cooperatives are owned by producers, consumers, workers, businesses, and other organizations, and by combinations of the above. They operate in all business sectors and in almost every country in the world.[28]

Unlike for-profit businesses, in which profitability is the primary measure of success, service to members is the first priority of cooperatives, but they also must maintain a level of profitability that allows them to operate sustainably over time.[29] By definition, the for-profit business model is radically different from the co-op model. To the extent that cooperatives become more dominant in society, the very nature of economic relations will change – from the primacy of profits to the primacy of service to members.

From a measurement perspective, the growth – or decline – of cooperatives is problematic, because there is no worldwide, longitudinal data set encompassing the many different types of cooperatives.

The United Nations sponsored the world's first global cooperative census in 2014,[30] providing benchmark data for future co-op censuses. The data in this census is from 2008 or later. Following are some key results:

- Almost 3 million cooperatives have about 2 billion memberships and clients – equivalent to over one-fourth of the world's population.[31]

- 12.6 million employees work in 770,000 cooperative offices and outlets.

- $20 trillion in cooperative assets generate $3 trillion in annual revenue[32]– equivalent to about 4 percent of the gross world product (GWP) or to the gross domestic product of the United Kingdom.[33]

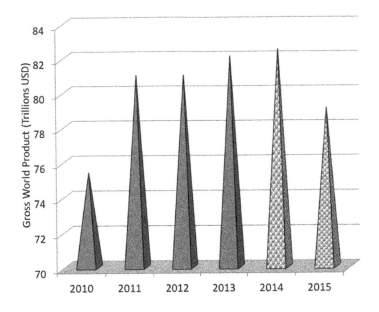

Figure 1.1 Global World Product, in real dollars.[33]

2018 update for the global co-op census

There has not been another co-op census since the one published in 2014, so we will have to continue to rely on the data from that census.

There are several longitudinal data sets for segments of the cooperative universe. Euricse[34] and the International Co-operative Alliance annually publish the *World Co-operative Monitor*, which provides information on the largest 300 co-ops and mutuals. These reports indicate that between 2010 and 2013, the revenue generated by the top 300 increased from about $2 trillion to $2.4 trillion – averaging a 5 percent increase per year over the four-year period.[35]

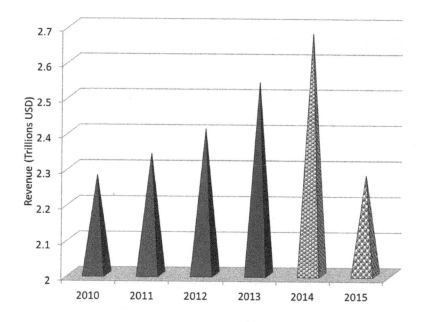

Figure 1.2 Revenue of the top 300 cooperatives.[36]

2018 update for the Co-op 300

Since the 2016 edition of this book, the *World Co-operative Monitor* has published two new reports in late 2016 and 2017 with data on the largest 300 co-ops in 2014 and 2015.[36] Converting the aggregate revenue of these co-ops to 2018 constant dollars, the trend of increasing revenue continued through 2014, but made a significant drop in 2015, as illustrated in Figure 1.2. We should not over-dramatize this one-year reduction in revenue. However, it will be important to watch results over the next several years.

The two co-op sectors with the largest numbers of memberships – insurance and financial services – have also experienced impressive growth in recent years.

The International Cooperative and Mutual Insurance Federation (ICMIF) publishes annual data on the state of its industry.

According to ICMIF, "The number of people protected by mutual and cooperative insurance (as members or policyholders) grew to 955 million in 2014, up from 923 million in 2013. As employers, mutual and cooperative insurers collectively employed 1.11 million people worldwide in 2014, a figure that has increased by more than 20 percent since before the global financial crisis (.92 million in 2007)." See Figure 1.3.

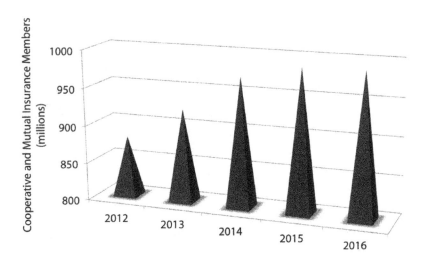

Figure 1.3 Cooperative and mutual insurance members/policyholders (millions).[138]

Credit unions, which comprise part of the financial cooperative sector, also have shown impressive growth in recent years. Worldwide, memberships grew from about 172 million in 2006 to 217 million in 2014 – an increase of about 26 percent or more than 3 percent per year. The increase in loan volume over the same period was 59 percent, an average of over 7 percent growth per year.[38]

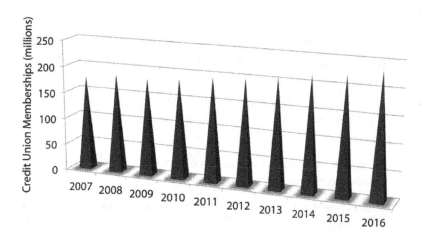

Figure 1.4 Credit union memberships (millions). [37]

2018 update for insurance co-ops/mutuals and for credit unions

Both credit unions and mutual insurance companies have continued to show growth in members since the publication of the 2016 edition of this book. The 2014 and 2015 data that were published in the past two years show a 4 percent annual membership growth rate for credit unions, and a 1 percent annual growth rate in members/policyholders for mutual insurance companies. Of particular note is that mutual insurance companies are on track to reach the billion-member/policyholder level in the next two years. These patterns of membership growth are presented in Figures 1.3 and 1.4.

The growth of members in both of these sectors was offset slightly by small decreases in financial performance. As with the top 300 cooperatives and mutuals, we will need to watch these financial data to see if they mark a new trend or a temporary blip.

Even though there is not yet comprehensive longitudinal data on cooperative performance, we can piece together a period of growth over the past few years. Some of the most important take-aways from these data sets are:

- Co-ops are a significant and growing part of the world economy – equivalent in economic power to the sixth-wealthiest country in the world.

- Co-ops are growing in the insurance sector at a faster rate than their for-profit competitors.

- We don't yet have a systematic, comprehensive means for measuring the growth or decline of global co-op business activity over time.

In summary, available co-op, credit union, and mutual insurance data indicate a recent drop in financial performance, but the long-term trend continues to be positive.

2. Large publicly traded corporations
2016 data

The largest 2,000 publicly traded companies in the world had revenue of over \$38 trillion in 2014.[38] This is equivalent to almost half of the gross world product (GWP), despite the fact that these businesses account for only 4 percent of all listed companies.[39] See Figure 1.5.

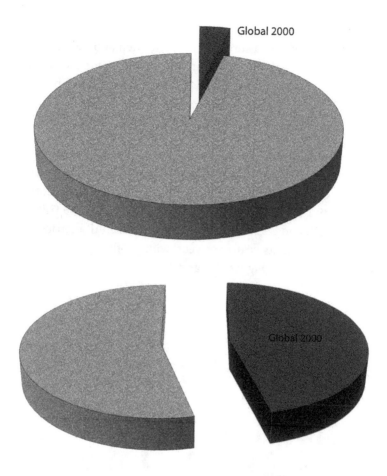

Figure 1.5 The largest 2000 companies are about 4% of all listed companies in the world, yet their revenue is almost half of the Gross World Product. [42]

Between 2003 and 2014, these large companies grew at a slightly faster pace than the GWP – an average annual increase of 6 percent over the 12-year period vs. 5.2 percent for the GWP.[40]

We concluded in the 2016 edition of this book that these large corporations dominate the world economy and that this domination has increased in the early 21st century.

2018 update

Figure 1.5 shows a surge, a drop, and then another surge in 2015, 2016, 2017, and 2018 in gross revenue for the Forbes 2000 companies – $41.2 billion, $36.5 billion, $36.3 billion, and $39.1 billion respectively.[41] This pattern is both in absolute terms and as a percentage of the gross world product.

"[The] 16th-annual Forbes Global 2000 list [published in June 2018] includes publicly-traded companies from 6 countries. Collectively, the companies on this list account for $39.1 trillion in sales, $3.2 trillion in profit, $189 trillion in assets, and $56.8 trillion in market value. All metrics are up double digits year-over-year, with profits up an impressive 28%."[42] See Figures 1.5 and 1.6.

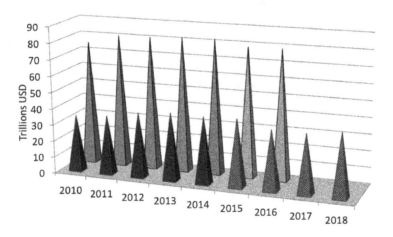

Figure 1.6 Forbes Global 2000 companies' sales revenue compared with Gross World Product, in real dollars.[41, 42]

Conclusions related to economic power

The most recently available data in 2018 indicate a slight decrease in the economic strength of cooperatives and a slight increase in the strength of large corporations compared to the 2016 data. But it is far too early to draw any long-term conclusions about these results. We will need to keep an eye on data in the coming years to determine whether or not new patterns are emerging.

And, we will need to continue to work on reducing the concentration of economic power regardless of short-term patterns. **Section C. Taking Action,** the final set of chapters in this book, provides practical steps that we as individuals, communities, and countries can take to democratize economic decision-making.

Chapter 2

Wealth and income

Wealth and income inequality in the world is extreme. There are a few positive signs related to the income of the very poor and to an emergent "world middle-class," but the super-wealthy are super-wealthier than ever and most of the planet's inhabitants are scraping by just above the bare minimum.

In this chapter, we present and analyze data on both wealth (which is the accumulation of money and other valuables over time) and on income (which is based on annual earnings and returns on investments).

Before digging into the data, let's review why we consider the degree of inequality to be an important indicator of whether or not we are moving toward a more cooperative society. Some people have argued that rewarding people for hard work, innovation, risk-taking, and other behavior is a benefit for society. That's probably true, but the extreme disparity in incomes and wealth within and across countries goes far beyond any explanation based on incentives and rewards for productivity.

Wealth

For example, one of the most dramatic statistics, reported by Oxfam International, is that in 2016, the 42 richest people in the world had as much wealth as the poorest half of the world's population – over 3½ billion people.[43] More broadly, in 2016, about 10% of households owned almost 90% of the wealth. One percent held 50%.[44] Figures 2.1 and 2.2.

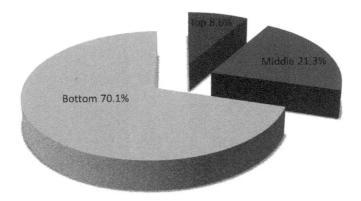

Population Percentile

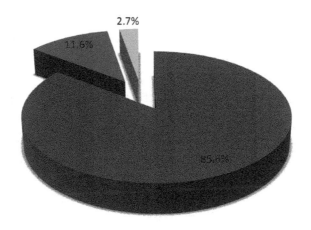

Wealth

Figure 2.1 The top 8.6% (those with $100,000+) own 85.6% of global wealth. The middle 21.3% ($10,000-$100,000) own 11.6%, whereas the bottom 70.1% (under $10,000) own just 2.7% of wealth.[44]

According to *Forbes*, there were a little over 2,000 billionaires worldwide in early 2018, an 18% increase in comparison to 2017.[45]

In reviewing Forbes 2017 data, Oxfam calculated that *just the increase in billionaire wealth ($762 billion) between 2016 and 2017* "could have ended global extreme poverty seven times over." Oxfam also calculated that 82% of the increase in global wealth went to the top 1%, and that none went to the bottom 50%.[46]

It is unimaginable to make an argument that these rich people are somehow thousands of times more productive and valuable than their poorer counterparts. There is strong evidence that the current levels of extreme inequality far exceed what can be justified by talent, effort, and risk-taking. Instead, they are more often the product of inheritance, monopoly, and crony connections to government.[47]

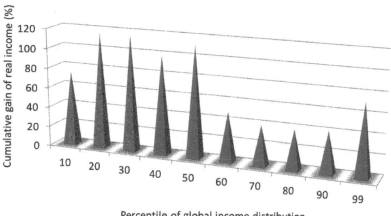

Figure 2.2 From 1980 to 2016, all income levels saw real per-capita income gains. At the high end, the global middle class saw gains of over 100%. At the low end, those with incomes at the 60-90-percentile level saw gains of under 50%. The poorest 10% and the richest 1% saw gains of about 75%.[49]

Income

Income disparities have shown a different pattern from that of wealth over the past three decades. An exhaustive study by Milanovic tracked income changes from the poorest 5% to the wealthiest 1%.[48] From 1980 to 2016, all income levels saw real per-capita income gains. At the high end, the global middle class saw gains of over 100%. At the low end, those with incomes at the 90th-percentile level saw gains of under 50%. The poorest 10% and the richest 1% saw gains of about 75%.[49]

High-income earners continue to dominate the world stage, but their margin of dominance is decreasing relative to the global middle class.

One criticism that has been leveled against this study is that Milanovic analyzed percent changes in income rather than absolute changes. Thus, a poor household increasing its income from $2 to $4 per day, and a million-dollar household doubling its annual income to $2 million would both be reported as experiencing a doubling of income. Recalculating income changes in absolute terms shows a much flatter curve for most of the world's households and a continuing rise in income for the top-earning households.[50]

Conclusions on wealth and income

Even though these data indicate some lessening of the dominance of high-income households in the world economy, the current reality is still one of extreme inequality of wealth and income.

Chapter 3

Conflict

The word "conflict" originates in Latin and old French with the meaning "armed encounter or battle."[51] In this chapter, we measure conflict by focusing on deaths resulting from war (both international and civil) and on intentional homicides.

The reason that we included conflict as one of the measures of movement toward or away from a more cooperative society is straightforward. In many ways, cooperation is the antithesis of conflict. As individuals, communities, and larger groupings of people, we can work together toward agreed-upon goals or we can fight with one another to achieve our own interests.

Thus, the extent to which there are violent deaths from conflict is a good indicator of whether or not we are becoming more or less cooperative.

In the 2016 edition of this book, we reported that there were far fewer worldwide deaths per year from domestic and international conflicts in the second half of the 20th and the beginning of the 21st century than there were in the first half of the 20th century. There were about 60 million deaths during World War II;[52] fewer than 10 per 100,000 in the second half of the 20th century; and on average, fewer than one death per 100,000 in the early part of the 21st century.[53] See Figure 3.1.

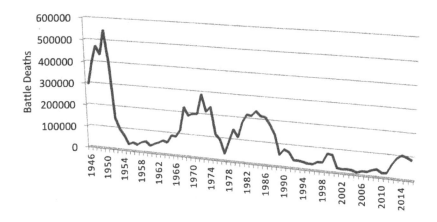

Figure 3.1 Battle deaths from 1946-2015. Uppsala Conflict Data Program (UCDP) & Peace Research Institute Oslo (PRIO).[139]

We also presented information on homicides. Global data on deaths from homicide were not reliably collected prior to 2000. Since then the annual, worldwide homicide rate dropped from about nine per 100,000 to six per 100,000 in 2012.[54] In comparison, some historians estimate the homicide rate in the 14th century at about 50 per 100,000.[55] See Figure 3.2.

We concluded that, based on these data, deaths from domestic and international conflicts have decreased dramatically, at least since the first half of the 20th century, and deaths from homicide have decreased in the first part of the 21st century and, probably, over a much longer period of time.[56]

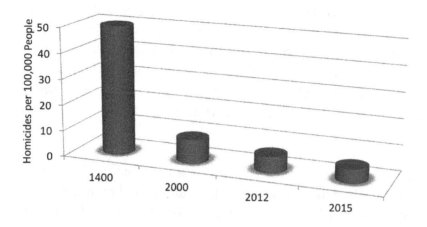

Figure 3.2 Global homicides per 100,000 people.[53, 54]

2018 update

There has been a slight uptick in deaths from war, especially civil war, in the first part of the 21st century. In 2016, the most recent year for which data were available, the rate of war deaths was a bit over 1 per 100,000 population. The peak year for battle deaths so far in the 21st century was 2014 with about 2 deaths per 100,000.[57,58]

The largest single cause of this recent rise in war deaths is the Syrian war.[59] This is a complex war because it combines elements of a multi-sided civil war with different factions receiving support from other countries and political groups. The protracted wars in Afghanistan and Iraq, again complex conflicts involving both international and domestic components, account for another large percentage of battle deaths in the early 21st century.[60] See Figure 3.1. Even with the slightly increased number of war deaths since 2000, the annual battle-death rate has remained far below the average rates in the first and second halves of the 20th century.[61]

Recent data on intentional homicides show a gradual decrease in the 21st century. There has been an almost steady decline in worldwide homicide rates since 2004 when there were just about

6 homicides per 100,000 of world population. In 2016, the most recent year for which we have data, there were slightly more than 5 homicides per 100,000.[62] That may not sound like much, but it represents about a 15% decline in the annual homicide rate.

What is also worthy of note is that the homicide rate is almost 5 times as high as the battle death rate in the 21st century so far.

In conclusion, violent death has decreased significantly since the mid-1900s. This is true both for war-related deaths and for intentional homicides. There is still a lot of conflict in the world, but we have made tremendous progress in reducing its lethal consequences in the last 70 years.

Chapter 4

Democracy

Democracy is not as easy to define and measure as one might think.

The Merriam-Webster online dictionary defines democracy as, "A government in which the supreme power is vested in the people and exercised by them directly or indirectly through a system of representation usually involving periodically held free elections."[63]

This definition seems straightforward enough, but as we will see in this chapter, several organizations have come up with very different results when rating countries around the world on their level of democracy. Despite these different measurement approaches, there is still a lot that we can say about international democratic trends over the past-century plus.

Even with these measurement issues, democracy remains an important indicator of whether or not the world is becoming more cooperative. The ability of most of the world's citizens to participate fairly in the governance of their countries is a prerequisite for a transition to the cooperative society.

In the 2016 edition of this book, we relied on two sources of data to analyze trends in world democracy: periodic reports by the Polity IV Project[64] (referred to below as "Polity") and the Economist Intelligence Unit[65] (referred to below as "EIU"). These reports diverge a bit in their analyses of past and current trends related to democracy. We review these differences below.

In 2016, we reported that Polity had analyzed data on democracy in the world all the way back to 1800. A summary of the project's findings from 1900 to 2014 is presented in Figure 4.1.

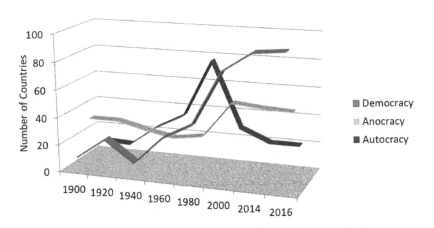

Figure 4.1 Democracy in the 20th and 21st centuries has grown in fits and starts. In 1900, there were about 10 countries with a Polity score of 8 or above. This number grew rapidly at the end of the 20th century, and in 2015 there were over 70 such countries.[64]

During that time, the number of democracies rose from 10 in 1900 to 94 in 2014. The combined number of autocracies and anocracies (countries that are neither fully democratic nor fully autocratic) stood at about 71 in 2014.[66] Thus, about 57 percent of the countries included in this analysis were democracies at that time.

The number of democracies accelerated after World War II, and again in the 1980s and early 1990s with the addition of some developing countries and of states that had been part of the Soviet Union.

Based on these data, the population of democratic countries was about the same as that of all non-democratic countries in 2014.[67]

The second graph (Figure 4.2) presented in the 2016 edition of this book indicated that the extent of democracy in the world, as measured by the EIU, had fluctuated, but not increased, between 2006 and 2015.[68]

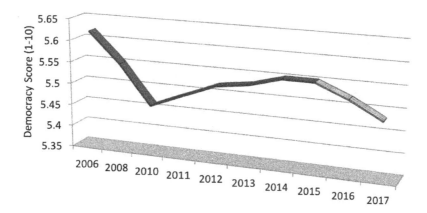

Figure 4.2 Over the past 11 years, the previous growth of democracy seems to have stagnated. On a 1-10 democracy scale created by EIU, the average world score fluctuated from 5.62 in 2006 to 5.46 in 2010 to 5.55 in 2014-15 to 5.48 in 2017. [68]

2018 update

The Polity and EIU datasets were both updated in late 2017.[69, 70] As in their earlier editions, both used multiple factors to measure the degree of democracy by country, and each had a database of over 160 countries. Both used a numerical scale to differentiate types of governance.

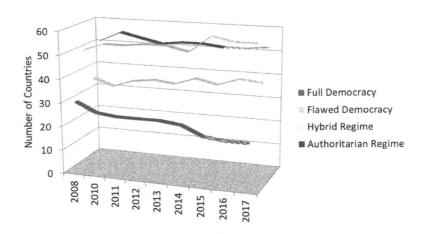

Figure 4.3 The number of full democracies has dropped from 2008 to 2017. [68]

The composite results of the Polity IV Project divide the world's countries into five categories:

Full Democracy	33
Democracy	63
Anocracy	46
Autocracy	21
Total	**163**

The Economist Intelligence Unit presents a classification of countries based on four categories:

Full Democracy	19
Flawed Democracy	57
Hybrid	76
Authoritarian	52
Total	**167**

What is most striking about these tables is the much higher number of democracies categorized by Polity than by the EIU – 96 vs. 76. Looking back over the past decade, this pattern of fewer countries receiving a democratic rating in the EIU dataset than in the Polity dataset is consistent.

The main explanation for this difference appears to be Polity's narrower focus on governance, including constraints on the executive branch, in calculating its democracy rating, and the EIU's use of a broader set of measures, including those related to civil liberties and political culture to classify a country's rating.

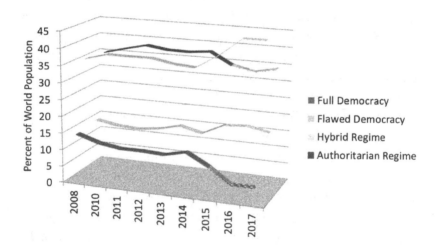

Figure 4.4 The percentage of people living under full democracies has also declined, with about half as many people (4.5%) living in a full democracy in 2017 compared with 2015 (8.9%). Still, about half of the world's population live in a full or flawed democracy.[68]

The EIU draws a significantly more negative conclusion about democratic trends than Polity over the last decade. Figure 4.4 shows a drop in the number of full democracies from 30 in 2008 to 19 in 2017 based on the EIU's analysis. This difference appears to reflect the broader, democracy-related criteria used by the

EIU. At the same time, however, the average governance rating of countries by the EIU fluctuates in a narrow range during the same time period – dropping from 5.6 to 5.5, (Figure 4.2) based on a 10-point rating scale. On this scale, 6 represents the lowest score for a "flawed democracy." So, according to the EIU, there has been a steep drop in the number of full democracies in the past few years, but the average governance rating in the world has stayed about the same.

Another difference between these two methodological approaches is their calculations of the percent of the world's population that lives in democratic countries. The EIU shows a fairly steady figure of just below 50% of humans living in democratic countries. Polity puts the figure at about 57%. Again, there is a significant difference in these ratings explainable primarily through Polity's narrower focus on governance and the EIU's broader definition of democracy.

Despite these differences, long-term trends clearly indicate a historical shift away from autocracy and toward democracy. The variation in recent years is relatively minor when this broader context is kept in mind. However, if the current instability and slippage related to democratic governance continues over the next few years, a new, negative trend away from full democratic governance may be emerging. But it is too early to draw such a conclusion at this time.

In any case, we have a long way to go before we can conclude that the world has become predominantly democratic.

Chapter 5

Population

We have added the measurement of population growth to the 2018 edition of the book. Thus, there is no comparison between 2016 data and 2018 data.

The world population reached 7.6 billion in 2018.[71] According to the United Nations, we are on track to slightly exceed 11 billion people by 2100.[72]

A rising population puts pressure on resources such as food, housing, health care, and a range of other goods and services, and tends to degrade the air, water, and land on which we depend. However, there is a myth about the consequences of an increasing world population that is important to note and debunk.

All the way back to Thomas Malthus' *An Essay on the Principle of Population*,[73] published in 1798, and continuing through Paul Ehrlich's *The Population Bomb* published in 1968,[74] and to an array of alarmists in the early 21st century,[75] there are those who take an apocalyptic view of population growth. None of the dire predictions of these prophets of doom have yet come to pass nor are they likely to, even if the world population reaches 11 billion in 2100.

That is not to say, however, that we should take lightly the United Nations' projected population growth of almost 45% between 2018 to 2100. This would not be a scenario for the end of human civilization, but it would be a lot less stressful on people and the planet if we were able to attain zero-population growth prior to reaching the 11-billion level.

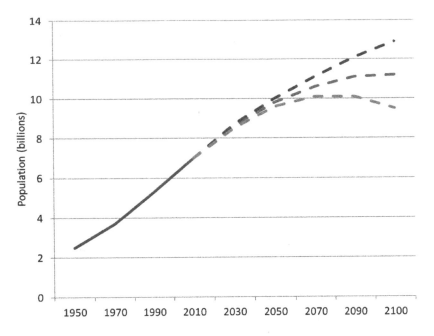

Figure 5.1 Historical and projected global population, with 95% confidence interval. [71]

There are several important things that we can do to improve our understanding of population trends and to "bend the population curve" downward.

The first one is to realize that the projected increase in population is an estimate, not a foregone conclusion. Thus, Figure 5.1 shows a range of trajectories – a high estimate of over 16 million people in 2100, the median estimate of about 11 million people, and a low estimate of about 7 million people. This is a huge range, reflecting the difficulty of estimating trends more than 80 years into the future. Many changes will affect the trajectory of the world's population between now and then – including reproductive health education, access to birth control, economic security, and cultural changes related to fertility.

A second factor is that the UN has a historical tendency to overestimate population growth. Its 1958 projection for the world's population in 2000 was on the high side by over 200 million people.[76] One reason for these population projection problems is a bias toward underestimating the decline in birth rates.[77] Even assuming greater sophistication in projection skills in the 21st century, it would not be surprising if the current estimate for 2100 were on the high side by half-a-billion people.

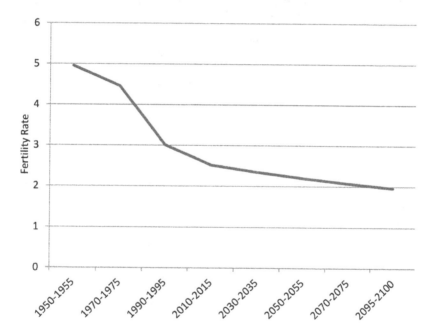

Figure 5.2 Historical and projected fertility rates.[140]

The above two points refer to measurement issues. But, what may be far more important factors affecting population growth are actions that people around the world take to change their reproductive behavior during the remainder of the century. Figure 5.2

shows birth-rate results beginning in 1955 and projected to the end of the 21st century.[78] The estimates in this graph are based on past trends and assumptions about future patterns. But these future patterns are things that we as individuals, families, and communities all the way up to international organizations will determine. We are not preordained to follow the pattern of birth rates depicted in the graph.

For example, based on survey data, there are more than 200 million women and couples who would like to limit the number of children they have, but don't have access to birth control education and contraceptives.[79] To the extent that improved reproductive health services become much more widely available in the next decade or so, there could be a significant reduction in the international birthrate. If these services continue to be available, the result could very well be a reduction in the number of kids born in the 21st century by well over a billion.

There is another behavioral factor at work that may have the biggest impact of all on the number of children who are born in this century. As people's standards of living and sense of security increase, we tend to have fewer kids. This pattern has been observed in families all over the world. It is often referred to as the "demographic transition." Its explanation is straightforward. In a low-income society, children are wealth. They help the family earn a living. As children get older, they support their parents. But when there is more money and a greater sense of security in the household, children often become an economic burden rather than a resource. They need healthcare, they need to go to school, they are another mouth to feed. As result, the traditional pattern of wanting to produce more kids to increase financial security gets turned on its head. The result is fewer kids per family. This transition often occurs very rapidly as a result of improved economic circumstances.

As the quality-of-life data in the 2016 version of this book reports, there has been a dramatic reduction in the number of people living in extreme poverty in the world. That number has been reduced by half from 1990 through 2015. It now stands at about 1.6 billion people.[80] One of the current UN Sustainable Development Goals is to eliminate extreme poverty by 2030.[81] If this goal is achieved or mostly achieved, the consequence may very well be several-hundred-million more women and couples deciding to limit the size of their families.

As the above data and analysis show, it is not a given that the world's population will reach 11 billion people by 2100. Many factors, especially assumptions about our future birth rate, may make significant changes in population growth over the next 80+ years. It is quite possible that the world will be able to reach zero-population growth below 11 billion people before 2100. There will be a further discussion and proposed action steps related to this topic in Chapter 13.

Chapter 6

Quality of life

One dictionary definition of quality of life is "the general well-being of a person or society, defined in terms of health and happiness, rather than wealth." [82]

Given this definition, quality of life is an important aspect of the cooperative society. The ability of the large majority of people around the world to live healthy, happy lives is a necessary component of a good society.

The United Nations Development Programme has been calculating an annual Human Development Index (HDI) since 1990. The index is a composite of life expectancy, education, and income-per-capita indicators. We used the HDI as the primary measure of worldwide changes in the quality of life in the 2016 edition.

As Figure 6.1 shows, the HDI has improved from about .57 to .71 over the past 25 years – about a 25 percent increase. Even after adjusting for income inequality, there has been a significant upward trend in the global quality of life. [83]

As a supplemental measure of change in the quality of life, we looked at several measures from the United Nations Millennium Development Goals over the same time period. Figure 6.2 shows that both extreme poverty and the number of deaths of children under five were reduced by 50 percent between 1990 and 2015. In addition, the number of children not enrolled in school decreased from 100 million to 57 million. The global maternity mortality ratio dropped from 382 to 210 per 100,000 live births.[84]

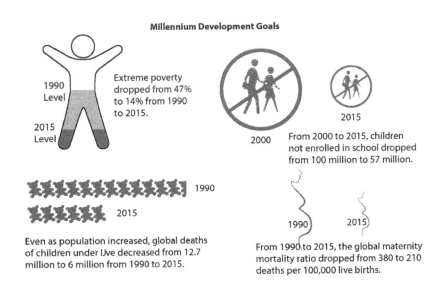

Millennium Development Goals

1990 Level

2015 Level

Extreme poverty dropped from 47% to 14% from 1990 to 2015.

2000

2015

From 2000 to 2015, children not enrolled in school dropped from 100 million to 57 million.

1990

2015

Even as population increased, global deaths of children under live decreased from 12.7 million to 6 million from 1990 to 2015.

1990

2015

From 1990 to 2015, the global maternity mortality ratio dropped from 380 to 210 deaths per 100,000 live births.

Figure 6.1 Selected Millennium Development Goal outcomes.[84]

2018 update

There is not much new information on quality-of-life issues to report in the 2018 edition of this book. The Human Development index has not been updated since 2016, and the Sustainable Development Goal Program which replaced the Millennium Development Goal Program in 2016 is still in the process of preparing its annual reporting system.

As a result, we have only one additional HDI report showing that in 2015, there was a minor improvement in the world HDI index – from .71 to .717[85] – and no new systematic data from the Sustainable Development Goal Program. One thing to note from the HDI report is that there has been a slower rate of improvement in the last few years compared to the first 20 years of measurement.

Despite the dearth of new data, there is clearly a long-term trend of improving quality of life around the world since 1990. We expect that by the next edition of *The Cooperative Society*, we will have quite a bit of new information that will confirm this long-term positive trend, or, less likely, throw it into question.

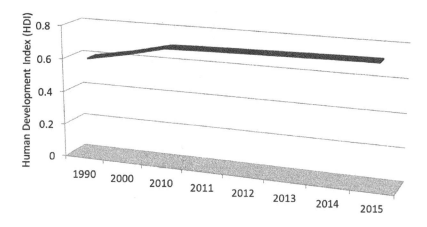

Figure 6.2 The Human Development Index (HDI) world average has grown since 1990. From 1990-2000 it grew at 0.71% per year. From 2000-2010 it grew at 0.82% per year. From 2010-2015 it grew at 0.61% per year. [85]

Chapter 7

Environment

We could have evaluated a range of ways in which human activity has increasingly degraded the planet's land, air, and water. Instead, we chose to focus on two negative impacts humans have had on the environment: species extinction (that is, killing off plants and animals that otherwise would still be around today), and climate change (raising the surface temperature of the earth by increasing the amount of carbon dioxide and related greenhouse gases in the atmosphere).

Species extinction

What is sometimes referred to as the "sixth great extinction" is the human-created demise of many of the world's plant and animal species – estimated by one study to be 1,000 times higher than would have occurred without human involvement.[86]

The last great extinction occurred about 66 million years ago.[87] At that time dinosaurs and many other plant and animal species died off in large numbers. Some scientists attribute this mass extinction to the aftermath of a large meteor striking the earth, and others to a period of high volcanic activity. In both scenarios, the atmosphere would have been choked with debris and greenhouse gases that would have been the death knell for many of Earth's species.[88]

And speaking of greenhouse gases, that is precisely what humans have been emitting into the atmosphere in increasing quantities since the beginning of the industrial era. Our use of fossil fuels to generate energy is the main factor taking a toll on plant and animal species today. There are other human-made factors besides greenhouse gas emissions that are threatening the planet's species as well. Just to name a few: habitat loss and degradation, overexploitation (hunting, harvesting, poaching, etc.), invasive species, and pollution.[89]

Figure 7.1 illustrates the increasing number of species that are being threatened by extinction since 1996. During that time the number of threatened species has increased from about 10,000 to over 25,000.[90] That's is a jump of over 150% in about 20 years.[91]

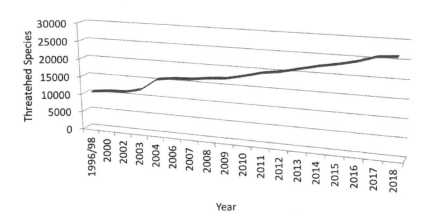

Figure 7.1 Red List of Threatened Species. There are an estimated 1,737,000 described species. In 2018, 5% (or 94,000) were evaluated for the Red List, and 26,000 (or 28%) of these were listed as threatened. For those groups that have been fully or almost fully evaluated (mammals, birds, gymnosperms) the percentage of threatened species ranges from 13 (birds) to 25 (mammals) to 40 (gymnosperms). The increase in threatened species includes both genuine reasons (new threats to species) and non-genuine reasons (artefacts of how the numbers have been calculated).[90]

Climate change

In the 2016 edition of *The Cooperative Society*, we reported on the increasing temperature of the earth's surface from 1890 (soon after such data first were reliably collected) to 2015. We chose this environmental indicator to illustrate what could become, in the 21st century, the worst human-made environmental disaster in the history of our species.

In this edition of the book, we update the information on climate change to 2017. The increase in temperature over the past 127 years, as shown in Figure 7.2, provides a stark illustration of how quickly we are heating up the surface of the planet.[92] The biggest culprit is the burning of fossil fuels, which spew carbon dioxide and other greenhouse gases into the atmosphere. The consequences are not only warmer temperatures, but also other negative changes, including increasing droughts, forest fires, rising ocean levels, other extreme weather events, and accelerated species extinction.[93]

Note that during the 127-year period for which data have been collected, the four warmest years are the last four, 2014-2017. The 10 warmest years are all since 1998.[94] So, the climate continues to get hotter, and the list of associated problems continues to get worse in the early 21st century.

In Chapter 14, we return to the topic of the environment, focusing on actions we can take to limit the damage we are doing to it. One topic in particular will be the commitments made by 195 countries to reduce their emissions of greenhouse gases, and how we as individuals and local communities can contribute to this goal.

Environmental Impact

The following NASA figures show average temperatures in each year compared with the 5-year average in different parts of the globe. Warmer-than-average temperatures are represented by yellows and reds. 2015 was the warmest year on record.

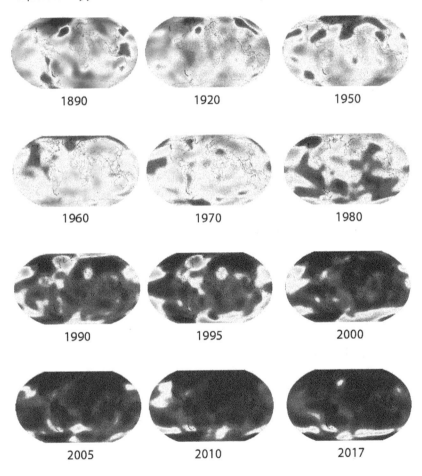

Figure 7.2 These NASA figures show average temperatures in each year compared with the 5-year average in different parts of the globe. Warmer-than-average temperatures are represented by yellows and reds. 2015 was the warmest year on record. [92]

Chapter 8

Cooperative society scorecard

Summary of trends as of 2018

The purpose of this chapter is to summarize the trends presented in the first seven chapters of the book, to provide an overview of whether or not we humans are moving toward or away from a more cooperative society, and to identify a set of targets for progress on these measures to be achieved by 2030. The seven measures presented in this section of the book provide mixed evidence for whether or not we are transitioning to the cooperative society.

1. **The economic power of large corporations is highly concentrated.**

   Large for-profit corporations continue to dominate the world economy which means they have a disproportionate impact on the decision-making that affects our lives and the health of the environment. As an illustration, the largest 2,000 publicly traded companies account for only 4% of all listed companies, but had a combined revenue of almost half the gross world product.

2. **Wealth and income are very unequally distributed.**

   The gap between wealthy and high-income individuals and households and the rest of us is in fact a chasm. One of the most telling statistic in Chapter 2 is that the increase in the wealth of billionaires between 2016 and 2017 was big enough to eradicate worldwide extreme poverty seven times over.

3. **The level of conflict around the world has dropped dramatically since the middle of the 20th century.**

   War deaths have decreased dramatically since the end of World War II, and homicides are down sharply since the beginning of the 21st century when systematic worldwide data was first collected. In 2016, war deaths were estimated at a little over one per 100,000 population per year, compared to over 20 deaths per 100,000 in the first half of the 20th century. Between 2000 and 2016, the rate of worldwide homicides per 100,000 decreased from nine to a little over five.

4. **Democracy has increased significantly since the beginning of the 20th century.**

   The number of democracies and the number of people living in democracies have grown, especially since the mid-20th century. According to one source, there are now 76 democracies (out of 167 countries), representing almost half of the world's population.

5. **The rating of population change is neutral.**

   The worldwide birthrate has been slowing steadily over the last several decades. However, current UN projections are that the population will grow from about 7.6 billion in 2018 to 11.1 billion in 2100. If we can slow the growth rate by improving incomes, health security, and knowledge about, and access to, birth control, we should be able to reach zero population growth before the end of the 21st century.

6. Quality of life has improved since 1990.

Both the Human Development Index and progress on the UN Millennium Development Goals indicate that fewer people around the world are living in extreme poverty, and that a variety of health and education indicators are also improving. The UN Sustainable Development Goals Program is intended to continue these improvements from 2016 through 2030.

7. Our despoliation of the environment may pose the biggest threat of all to our species and planet.

The largest of these negative impacts is our continued dumping of carbon dioxide and other greenhouse gases into the atmosphere. The surface temperatures of the earth in 2014-2017 were the four warmest since reliable measurement began in the late 1800s. The Paris Climate Change Agreement is intended to reduce these greenhouse gas emissions between now and 2030. We will monitor how this works out.

Combined impact of the seven measures on movement toward a cooperative society

Using a simple additive approach, the "score" of these measures is:

- 3 negatives – concentrated economic power, unequal distribution of wealth and income, and damage to the environment

- 3 positives – reduced conflict, increased democracy, and improved quality of life

- 1 neutral – population growth

Thus, in some ways, we are moving toward a more cooperative society. In other ways, we aren't. And in terms of population change, there is no clear pattern yet.

2030 targets

We have set a target for each measure to be achieved by 2030. Each target is intended to indicate progress to be achieved by that year. This approach is similar to the UN Sustainable Development Goals and the goals of the Paris Climate Agreement, both of which have 2030 targets.

Measure	2030 Target
1. Economic power	Reduction of the combined revenue of the Forbes 2000 as a percentage of GWP from 43% in 2016 to under 40% in 2030
2. Wealth and income inequality	Wealthiest 10% to decline from 90% ownership of all wealth in 2016 to 80% in 2030
3. Conflict	Two targets: a. Reduction in battle deaths to fewer than 1 per 100,000 b. Homicides reduced to 4 per 100,000
4. Democracy	55% of the world's population living in democratic countries, an increase from 50% in 2016
5. Population	World population of 8.5 billion in 2030 instead of UN-projected 8.6 billion
6. Quality of life	Human Development Index of .80, increased from 2015 level of .72
7. Environment	The temperature of the earth's surface between 1.5°C and 2°C above the pre-industrial level

The next section of the book, **C. Taking action**, outlines actions that we as individuals, communities, countries, and international organizations can take to realize the targets summarized above, and move closer to the creation of a cooperative society.

Section C:
Taking action

Taking action

As human beings, we have the power to shape the world in which we live. Because of this ability, we can act strategically to evolve into a more humane society.

We can take actions to reinforce the positive trends and to counter the negative ones identified in Chapters 1 through 7. The recommendations in Chapters 9 through 15 primarily focus on changes we can make by 2030, the target dates for both the Paris Accord on Climate Change and the UN's Sustainable Development Goals.

The process of change starts with each of us as individuals. We may feel powerless to make positive changes in the world. But we aren't.

Think about all the ways we interact with one another. We are family members, students, workers, unemployed, or retired. We have friends and neighbors. We live in a community. Depending on the country in which we live, we have the power to cast a meaningful vote. We are consumers. We may have funds to invest or time to volunteer. We may have one or more causes that we care about – for example, healthcare, an environmental issue, or something else. We may be a volunteer for a local activity – feeding the hungry, providing assistance to the elderly, tutoring kids, or another activity.

Every one of the roles we play in our communities presents opportunities for changing the world – not necessarily on a grand scale, but in small ways. Small changes add up.

Three recent examples

Malala Yousafzai, a Pakistani high school student

At the age of 15, Malala Yousafzai, a Pakistani high school student, was gravely wounded in an assassination attempt because of her activities in support of female education. She survived the attack and went on to form the Malala Fund, "…working for a world where every girl can learn and lead without fear." *She was the youngest recipient ever to receive the Nobel Peace Prize, in 2014.*[95]

Marjory Stoneman Douglas High School, Parkland, Florida

Seventeen students were killed at a high school in Parkland, Florida, in February 2018. What was the student response? To organize protests in favor of stricter gun laws to reduce the likelihood of this type of tragedy happening again. They didn't just organize in their own community; they and other students organized protests in dozens of cities around the country, including Washington, D.C. Within the next few weeks, Florida and three other states passed laws limiting access to guns, at least in part due to the Parkland student activism.[96]

The #MeToo Movement

The #MeToo Movement, founded by Tarana Burke in 2006, skyrocketed in visibility beginning in October 2017 after dozens of women publicly accused Harvey Weinstein, a famous movie producer, of sexually abusing them. Several months later, thousands of women in the United States and in other countries have been outing sexual predators under the banner of the MeToo hashtag. In many cases the accused are losing their jobs and being tried for their offenses.[97, 98, 99]

In all three of these examples, a small number of people took action. These initial steps became the basis for large-scale efforts for reform.

The following chapters provide examples of how we can take action to make improvements in all aspects of society analyzed in Chapters 1 through 7.

Chapter 9

Decentralize economic power

Increasing democracy and accountability in economic decision-making can be pursued in a variety of ways: Patronizing locally owned small businesses; supporting social enterprises that put service before profit; decreasing the economic and political power of large, for-profit businesses; and strengthening and creating businesses that are democratically controlled by their members.

1. Grow cooperative businesses

The data presented in Chapter 1 indicate that the number of cooperatives in the world is approaching three million, and the number of co-op memberships is about two billion. We believe that there are numerous opportunities to create additional co-ops and to double the number of cooperative memberships by 2030. To achieve this expansion, we've identified six opportunities:

- **Get involved.**
  Join a co-op. Form a co-op. Play an active role in a co-op. For example, hundreds of millions of people around the world have access to credit unions (and similar financial co-ops) and insurance co-ops and mutuals. Services at these co-ops are usually as affordable as, or less expensive

than, their non-co-op competitors. So, join one. If you don't have easy access to one, explore the possibility of working with a group of people to establish a branch or form a new one. Check out the Co-opLaw e-resource library online for ideas and information.[100]

• Improve measurement of co-ops and co-op performance.

Without systematically measuring the number of cooperatives and related variables over time, it is not possible to tell whether the co-op movement is increasing or decreasing in size and sustainability. This lack of information creates a fundamental problem. How can we increase the role of co-ops in the world if we don't know how many there are or what they are doing? Good data and analysis are prerequisites to good planning. Research on co-ops, including a periodic, global census, is a necessity for effectively planning their long-term growth.

A high priority for the co-op movement should be the support, development, and use of such measures. The Committee for the Promotion and Advancement of Cooperatives (COPAC) has recently begun a process to fill this measurement gap.[101]

• Improve the legal and regulatory environment for co-ops.

The quality of cooperative laws, regulations, and regulatory systems varies dramatically from one country to the next. All countries should have co-op laws, regulations, and enforcement practices that are consistent with the seven cooperative principles.[102]

The Cooperative Law Committee of the International Co-operative Alliance explores ways to improve co-op laws and regulations throughout the world. It holds international forums and other activities on this topic.[103]

- **Strengthen community-level, national, and international support for cooperatives.**

  Because co-ops are democratically controlled businesses that are designed to meet the needs of their members and their communities, one would think they would be treated as a strategic complement to government programs and community-development initiatives. However, there is tremendous variation in the extent to which this complementary relationship exists in practice. Strengthening the connection between co-ops and their communities is already one of the seven cooperative principles. However, improving this community connection needs to become a higher priority for co-ops and their apex organizations in the years ahead, building on such initiatives as the International Co-operative Alliance's "Blueprint for a Cooperative Decade."[104]

- **Improve cooperative development and financial assistance.**

  Cooperatives don't start themselves. They usually need outside help in order to develop business plans, secure financing, and operate effectively. However, there are far too few cooperative development organizations and co-op-oriented financial institutions, especially in developing countries, to carry out these startup and support services.[105] Technical assistance providers themselves need organizational, legal, financial, and training support. Some of this can come from within the established co-op community, but there is an important role for governmental and foundation support, as well. Development assistance is often the missing link between a good co-op business opportunity and the establishment of a co-op to address that opportunity.

- **Develop targeted strategies for co-op sectors, countries, and job creation opportunities.**

   Doubling the number of co-op memberships by 2030 can happen only if the factors such as better measurement; improved legal environments; community, governmental, and international support; and ongoing cooperative development assistance all increase dramatically.

   In addition, we need to think strategically about where to focus development resources. For example, insurance co-ops and mutuals and financial cooperatives, have shown systematic development strategies that have resulted in significant growth over the past few years. The same type of approach should be applied in other co-op sectors.

The expansion of cooperative businesses – especially the doubling of cooperative memberships – won't just happen. It has to be planned, funded, implemented, evaluated, and revised between now and 2030. For this to happen, the International Co-operative Alliance and others in the co-op community should take the lead development role.

For more ideas, see "Cooperative business opportunities" in the appendix.

2. Expand social enterprises

As we discussed in Chapter 1, social enterprises are businesses that put services before profit. Some co-ops meet the definition of social enterprises. Many of the points mentioned above apply to social enterprises as well as to co-ops.

We can support the formation and operation of these businesses in our communities. For example, a number of these enterprises are involved in recycling and reusing clothing, building materials, furniture, and other items. We can support them by donating, by purchasing, by volunteering, and in other ways.

3. Large for-profit corporations

When it comes to big businesses and politics, money talks – and it has a very loud voice. The business lobby in Washington, D.C., has a budget that is greater than those of both the U.S. Senate and House of Representatives combined.[106] Ultimately, the voices of voters and their elected representatives are the best way to counterbalance the economic and political power of big business – within countries and internationally.

To what extent is this likely to happen in the next 12 years?

One encouraging fact is that something similar has happened before. At the end of the 19th and beginning of the 20th century, the U.S. economy was dominated by what were then called "trusts" – monopolies and oligopolies of large corporations that distorted the operation of the market. Beginning with the Sherman Antitrust Act of 1890, and followed by additional legislation over several decades, "trust busting" broke up and reduced the power of these corporations.[107]

Today, the U.S. Federal Trade Commission is charged with preventing "mergers and acquisitions that are likely to reduce competition and lead to higher prices, lower-quality goods or services, or less innovation."[108]

The challenge is different today from what it was 100 years ago. Anticompetitive behavior is still a problem around the world. But the domination of the world economy by large corporations in the early 21st century is not just a matter of unfair competition. The primary threat comes from the simple fact that the profit-motivated decisions of these giant businesses often wreak havoc on our social, economic, and environmental well-being.

We saw in the Great Recession, which officially lasted from December 2007 to June 2009, how a few large banks had the power to put the entire international economy into crisis because of their reckless behavior in creating highly leveraged investment instruments tied to subprime mortgages. When the housing bubble burst in the United States, the value of these instruments plummeted, leaving the banks and global investors holding worthless or near-worthless paper.[109] For example, the banks of Iceland virtually bankrupted the country's economy, in large part because of their heavy investment in subprime-mortgage derivatives.[110]

Also, in order to protect their profits, many large fossil-fuel companies have consistently downplayed the impact of carbon dioxide and other human-caused greenhouse-gas emissions on global temperatures and related adverse climate changes. These denials, and the lobbying that has accompanied them, have slowed the response of the U.S. and the international community to the climate-change crisis. This slow response has meant greater damage to the planet's ecology and much higher costs for remediating that damage. The primary reason for the delays and higher costs: bolstering the short-term profits of fossil-fuel companies.

This is not unlike the denials by the tobacco companies during the last half of the 20th century that cigarettes and other tobacco products cause cancer. These decades of stonewalling have resulted in tens, possibly hundreds, of millions more deaths than would have occurred had regulatory actions and warnings to the public begun earlier.[111]

The underlying problem is that basing decision-making in the world economy on the self-interest of large corporations has the effect of bombarding us with one environmental, social, and economic crisis after another.

This paradigm has to change – which takes us back to the question of how to curb the size and power of these corporations. We need a new set of antitrust laws on a country-by-country basis and on a world scale. And we need enforcement of these laws.

Wresting control of the international economy from big business will not occur in one sweeping action. It will take hundreds of small steps – popular protest movements, country-by-country legislation, and international agreements – to put the well-being of people and the planet ahead of profits.

All of the following mechanisms will need to come into play:

More stringent regulations that prevent and punish anti-competitive behavior and require corporations to internalize costs of doing business that now are dumped on the rest of us, such as greenhouse-gas emissions and other pollutants; health costs related to smoking, obesity, and other unhealthy problems fostered by some companies; and financial consequences of disrupting international markets.

Elimination of tax havens and other international tax-avoidance schemes. These actions, which will require international cooperation to address, apply to wealthy individuals as well as corporations.

Graduated corporate income taxes based on the size and profitability of businesses. This would serve as a disincentive for businesses to become too large.

Strict limits on corporate involvement in lobbying and the electoral process. The structure of these limitations will vary from country to country. In the United States, one of the most egregious problems is the ability of large businesses and other incorporated entities to pour virtually unlimited amounts of money into influencing political campaigns. For example, the 2010 Supreme Court ruling in favor of Citizens United, a conservative organization that had challenged limits on political advertising, affirmed this kind of corporate spending as a right of "free speech." Overturning this Supreme Court decision will require either a reversal by a future Supreme Court or a constitutional amendment.[112]

We also can learn from the lessons provided by countries that historically have done a better job of keeping economic and political inequalities at a low level – the Scandinavian countries, for example.[113] In addition, on an international scale, trade and aid policies by more-progressive countries can be used to provide incentives to, and impose sanctions on, countries that foster inequality, authoritarian rule, and/or carry out other domestic policies harmful to their citizens.

Chapter 10

Reduce inequality in household income and wealth

What can we as individuals do to reduce income and wealth inequality? At first glance, it seems like an insurmountable task. The only way that it becomes achievable is that we work with others to reform the tax systems and spending priorities of our elected officials. For some of us who don't live in democracies, a prior step to tax and spending reform is organizing for the right to fair elections and accountable leaders.

Thomas Piketty received broad international attention for his book, *Capitalism in the Twenty-First Century*, first published in 2013, in which he analyzed wealth and income around the world, especially during the latter half of the 20th century and the beginning of the 21st century. His analysis concluded that the main cause of worsening inequality is the greater ability to increase future wealth through the investment of current wealth, rather than through wages and salaries. He recommended that the best way to reduce the concentration of wealth would be to tax it uniformly in all countries of the world.[114]

Such a joint world-wide taxation scheme does not appear to be a realistic option. However, on a country-by-country basis, voters and elected officials can institute progressive tax reform that eventually would approximate the kind of worldwide impact that Piketty calls for.

Voting for progressive tax reform is the primary recommendation of this chapter, and the most effective way to reduce within-country inequality. The underlying principle is that the higher your income and the greater your wealth, the higher proportion of income and wealth taxes you should pay.

Within a country, the taxation system and the array of economic- and social-support programs are the key factors that influence income and wealth inequality. Progressive income and wealth taxes reduce the gap between the rich and the rest of us. At the same time, they generate revenue that can be used to improve the economic conditions of a large majority of citizens through a variety of means: access to affordable health care; education; food and housing assistance payments; and retirement benefits. Several northern European countries have done a very good job of creating societies with relatively low inequality and a high quality of life, with progressive taxes playing a key role.[115]

International and between-country inequality is a more difficult problem to address. How do we go about reducing the inequality between the citizens of France and those of Burkina Faso? Part of the answer derives from trade and aid policies between the two countries. Do their trade agreements provide reasonable access by Burkina Faso to French markets? Does the aid relationship better prepare Burkina Faso and its citizens to compete in the international marketplace?

These types of questions need to be asked for all kinds of bilateral and multilateral relationships between and among poor countries and wealthy ones. There is no "one-size-fits-all" answer.

Even with international trade and aid issues, we as individuals play a role, particularly as voters who emphasize the election of leaders with progressive agendas related to the world economy.

We as individuals can also affect inequality on an international level by the way we choose to consume goods and services. For example, there are "certified" agricultural and other products that are produced by farmers and workers in developing countries for which they are paid a fair percentage of the value of their products. When we shop, we can purchase these products,[116] and, if they are not available, we can encourage our co-ops and other retailers to carry them.

The Commitment to Development Index ranks 27 of the wealthiest countries in terms of a variety of aid- and trade-related measures. In 2017, Denmark ranked first in terms of the overall impact of its policies on developing countries. France was fourth, the UK was 7th and the U.S., the richest country in the world, was a lowly 23rd. Japan was the worst at 27th.[117]

This type of index measures and reports comparative performance. There is no enforcement power behind the evaluations, although the ranking system can be used to shame the poor-performing countries into increasing their fairness, generosity, and effectiveness.

It is worth considering a more robust use of this and similar rating systems. An international-development certification program could be used to provide incentives and sanctions based on each country's rating. The program could be divided into several categories related to the development level of the country being evaluated, for example, using a measure of gross domestic product (GDP) per capita. The ratings of high-GDP countries would emphasize measures similar to the Commitment to Development Index. Countries with low GDP per capita would feature variables that indicate how effectively they use trade and aid assistance. These measures would include past performance on development projects, level of corruption, level of democracy, and similar measures.

Chapter 11

Reduce conflict

Homicides

There is a huge variation around the world in annual rates of homicide. The highest rates occur in countries involved in drug production and transportation. Gangs often attempt to kill each other off, forcibly recruit young people, and cause collateral damage. Many of the migrants attempting to enter the United States through Mexico in the spring and summer of 2018 were fleeing gang violence in Honduras, Nicaragua, and El Salvador. The United States would be far better off working with these countries to reduce the drug problem rather than using draconian measures to keep these migrants out of the country.

The U.S. has its own homicide problem. It is the only developed country in the world that has a lax gun-control program, and, not surprisingly, also has the highest homicide rate among developed countries.[118] Thus, in the U.S., the best way to reduce homicides in the long term is to restrict access to guns, especially handguns and assault-style weapons. There is a myth that banning assault-style weapons is the key to solving the problem. However, the vast majority of homicides were committed using handguns.[119]

However, politicians have been reluctant to put limitations on gun ownership in the United States, partly because of contributions from the National Rifle Association, and partly because there is a warped value in the U.S. that the "right to bear arms" somehow means that any restriction on gun ownership is an infringement on a constitutional right. As voters, U.S. citizens can demonstrate that owning a gun and the type of gun one owns need to be balanced with other human rights.

What can we do to reduce homicides in our own neighborhoods and communities? With or without guns, most homicides occur between family members or between other people who know each other. We can encourage people who are experiencing domestic abuse to seek out help. We can do the same with friends and acquaintances who are abusing drugs and alcohol. It is also a big help if there is a positive police presence in the community where people feel comfortable interacting with them. Unfortunately, in some neighborhoods there is a strong antagonistic relationship between police and community members rather than one based on a shared goal of making life peaceful and secure. Elected officials, police, and local residents can all work to achieve the latter goal. In the bigger picture, this cooperative approach will reduce violence.

War and genocide

As the data in Chapter 3 show, there is a significant trend toward fewer deaths from conflict from the first half of the 20th century through the early 21st century. This is despite the Rwanda genocide in 1994 and the wars in Afghanistan, Iraq, and Syria in the first part of the 21st century. Over 100 million people died during the First and Second World Wars. The number of deaths after World War II peaked in 1950 at over 500,000, primarily a result of the Korean War. The number in 2016 was under 100,000 deaths, most as a result of the war in Syria.

There are still far too many war deaths in recent years, but the death rate is much lower than the 20th-century average. What can we do to bring the number down further?

Much of the violence in the world today centers on the Middle East and Afghanistan, and involves a combination of sectarian conflict, primarily between Sunni and Shia factions of Islam, within and between countries; a proliferation of terrorist organizations (which overlaps with the conflicts within Islam); and popular protests to move from authoritarian to more democratic rule.

Developed countries, most notably the United States, have been active in attempting to assist the Afghan government to defeat or reach a political settlement with the Taliban. Developed countries have invaded Iraq and then attempted to help transform that country into a democracy, and they have played a support role in attempting to oust the Assad regime in Syria. As of this writing, none of these interventions is going very well, although ISIS has lost most of its foothold in Syria and Iraq.

Outside military intervention clearly has not yet led to increased stability or democracy in this region. What will? Following are four ideas on this question:

- Political and religious reform must be led from within the region and within specific countries of the region, not imposed from outside.

- As democratically oriented protests transition into fledgling democracies – Tunisia, for example – they need to receive economic and political support from developed countries.

- Middle Eastern countries with authoritarian regimes should receive incentives from the West to increase human rights and democracy, coupled with trade and aid restrictions if they continue to operate as internally oppressive regimes and/or as aggressors against other countries.

- Learn from recent history that military intervention has not been a very successful route to democracy.

The sanctions against Iran by European Union countries and the U.S. played a major role in securing a commitment by Iran to cease its development of nuclear weapons.[120] However, in 2018, President Trump announced his intention to withdraw the United States from this agreement. Thus, it is not clear what will happen next.

Similar incentives and sanctions can help to reduce conflict and increase democracy in other parts of the world as well, for example, the end of apartheid in South Africa in the early 1990s.[121]

Chapter 12

Expand democracy

From the data presented in Chapter 4, we learned that between 46% and 59% (depending on which organization is doing the analysis) out of about 165 countries have full or "flawed" democracies. Again, depending on the source, between 50 and 57% of the world's population lives in democratic countries. In either case, this represents a huge increase in democracy from the beginning of the 20th century. At that time, there were only an estimated 10 democracies.

So, how do we expand democracy into the rest of the world?

There has been a groundswell of populist movements in the past few years calling for increased accountability by political leaders and economic elites. These include the Arab Awakening in over a dozen countries in North Africa and the Middle East in 2010 and the decades-long democracy struggle in Myanmar. There have been similar, if less visible, movements worldwide. But it has not proven easy to transition from protest movement to the formation of a democratic government. Of the 12 or so movements that were part of the Arab Awakening, only the one in Tunisia has resulted in the formation of a democratic government, to date.

History shows that the transition from authoritarianism to democracy usually is not quick or easy. On the other hand, it also shows that, measured over the past century, the transition has occurred on a dramatic scale. Democracy also has tended to grow in fits and starts. For example: the immediate post-World War II period, the emergence of former colonial countries in the late 1950s through early '70s, and the dissolution of the Soviet Union in the late 1980s and early '90s.

As individuals, we have the power to protest and to vote in support of increased democracy in our own countries and abroad.

Democratization can be accelerated in other countries by the policies of governments and economic leaders in democratic countries. Some developed countries, for example the members of the European Union, include criteria for democracy and human rights in their trade and aid policies. In other words, they use their economic and political relationships with other countries to provide incentives for democracy, and sanctions against repression.[122] Those of us who live in democratic, developed countries can vote for elected officials who support both domestic and international democracy.

There are other ways that we, as individuals, can "vote" for democracy – that is by the way we make decisions as consumers, financial donors, and volunteers. We can join boycotts of goods that are produced in ways that are not respectful of human rights and democracy. We can also support the purchase of food products and other items from developing countries that are produced under "fair-trade" or similar agreements. We can also donate to causes that support democracy and volunteer our time to support them. As mentioned in an earlier example, there was a boycott of South African products that lasted over 40 years until apartheid ended in the early 1990s.[123]

For democratization to succeed, however, as we saw in the Arab Awakening, there must be strong support for it within the countries that are attempting to achieve it. In some cases, as in South Africa, the base of support for democracy must be built up over decades.

Most of us are unaware that China has had a national policy since 1998 of having villagers elect their local councils through secret ballots. About two-thirds of Chinese adults are eligible to vote in these elections. This local-level democracy by no means indicates that China is on the verge of democratic elections at the national level. However, during the next 10 to 20 years, this local electoral process may lead to a greater role for democracy in the country.[124] Since China is home to almost 20 percent of the world's population, such a transition would be an extraordinary leap forward for democracy.

Chapter 13

Reduce population growth

At the rate of growth projected by the United Nations, the world population will grow from about 7.6 billion in 2018 to 8.6 billion in 2030. As we pointed out in Chapter 5, there is nothing immutable about this growth rate. There are many things that we as individuals, communities, countries, and international organizations can do to "bend the curve" downward.

In Chapter 9, we set a goal of reducing the rate of population growth over the next 12 years by 10%, so that instead of having 8.6 billion people on the planet, we would have 8.5 billion.

How might we go about achieving this goal?

Let's consider this five-part strategy:

1. Provide more education on reproductive health.

The World Health Organization has identified inadequate access by teenagers to reproductive health education as a key health and population problem, especially in developing countries. Consequences of a lack of knowledge by adolescents about birth control and other aspects of reproductive health include: unwanted teen pregnancies, unsafe abortions, and an increase in sexually-transmitted diseases.[125]

2. Increase access to birth control.

The first thing to recognize is that survey data show that over 200 million women and couples who currently don't have access to contraceptives, would like to have access.[126] Note that if each one of these individuals and couples had one fewer child as a result of greater availability of contraceptives in the next 12 years, this would translate into 200 million fewer children by 2030. This change alone would result in a reduction of the world's population in 2030 from 8.6 billion to 8.4 billion – twice the reduction of our projected goal.

3. Eliminate extreme poverty.

One of the quality-of-life goals reviewed in Chapter 6 is the United Nations Sustainable Development Goal to eliminate extreme poverty by 2030. This is also a population goal because when people's economic conditions are improved, they tend to have fewer children.

4. Increase incomes for those above the extreme poverty line.

As with the elimination of extreme poverty, increased financial security farther up the economic chain also results in reduced birth rates.

5. Improve other aspects of the social safety net.

It is not just increased economic security that has an impact on reducing population growth. There is a range of factors associated with increased well-being that have an impact on reducing birth rates – for example improved access to health care services, social security systems, and other improvements in social conditions.

It's one thing to list a variety of ways to reduce the rate of population growth, and another to implement such changes. However, by dovetailing with already-established programs such as the World Health Organization's reproductive health initiatives, the Gates Foundation, and the Sustainable Development Goal program of the United Nations, a 10% reduction in the birth rate by 2030 is a realistic goal.

Chapter 14

Improve the quality of people's lives

How can we as individuals take on the monumental task of making life better for almost 8 billion people around the world? For the most part, by taking small actions as citizens, voters, members of religious and nonprofit organizations, and consumers. Through these roles we can take actions to support the right of people in every country to have decent lives in keeping with the United Nations Universal Declaration of Human Rights (summarized in Section B of the book).

As citizens, we can express our views on universal human rights. As voters, we can work to elect political leaders who are committed to a decent standard of living for all. As members of religious and nonprofit organizations, we can donate time and money in furtherance of human rights. As consumers, we can make choices in what we purchase that benefit low-income producers and workers (for example products that are certified Fair Trade).

The quality-of-life data presented in Chapter 6 reveal that there has been significant worldwide progress on several key quality-of-life measures in the past 25 years. The Human Development Index has improved by almost 25 percent since 1990. Even when adjusting for inequality by country, there has been substantial improvement. Performance on the Millennium Development Goals over the same time period also has been positive. For example, both extreme poverty and deaths of children under five years old were reduced by about half.

Despite indications of progress, there is still a long way to go to achieve an adequate quality of life for the world's 7.6 billion inhabitants. In 2015, the members of the United Nations unanimously approved the 2030 Agenda for Sustainable Development as a follow-up to the Millennium Development Goals.[127] This UN initiative runs from 2016 to 2030. It contains 17 goals divided into 169 measurable targets. For example, the first and probably most ambitious, is "to end poverty in all its forms everywhere." The measurement of this goal is based on the elimination of extreme poverty, which is currently defined as $1.90 per day (based on 2011 dollars). Put another way, it is "the inability to meet basic consumption needs on a sustainable basis."[128]

Even though these goals are ambitious, the successful track record of the Millennium Development Goals provides evidence that this new initiative for improving the quality of life on a worldwide scale has good potential.

However, it is still too early to tell whether or not there have been measurable benefits from the follow-up of the Sustainable Development Goals program. By the next edition of the book, we should be able to provide a progress report on this program.

Chapter 15

Create a more sustainable environment

1. Reduce global warming

International and national levels

The Agenda for Sustainable Development wasn't the only historic agreement reached by the United Nations in 2015.[129] UN members also adopted the Paris Agreement on Climate Change in December of that year.[130]

Scheduled to take effect in 2020, almost every country in the world is developing plans to reduce their greenhouse-gas emissions to prevent the surface temperature of the world from increasing by more than 2°C above its pre-industrial level by 2030 and, preferably, limiting the increase to 1.5° C.[131] This reduction in emissions is intended to avoid catastrophic consequences in global warming and related severe weather events.

The major exception to adherence to this agreement is the United States, which has announced that it will pull out of the agreement in 2020. However, a coalition of U.S. states, cities, businesses, universities, and others has formed an organization called We Are Still In. They intend to meet the goals for reduced greenhouse-gas emissions that the federal government has abdicated. [132]

The Paris Agreement on Climate Change is a decentralized one, in which each country is planning and implementing its own set of strategies for reducing and offsetting emissions. There are risks in such an approach, because there is no guarantee that all countries will make good-faith or effective efforts to address climate-change problems. On the other hand, given the international politics surrounding issues related to global warming, this agreement was probably the only option that could have received unanimous approval.

On the positive side, there will be careful international monitoring of the effects of each country's climate-change strategy, and in 2023 and 2028, national climate-change plans will be revised to increase the likelihood that the goal of limiting the surface temperature of the world to between 1.5°C and 2°C above the preindustrial level will be achieved by 2030.

Individual and local actions

What can we as individuals do to create a more sustainable environment? Unlike improving the quality of life for people around the world, discussed in Chapter 14, there are a number of relatively simple, straightforward things that we can do to make the planet more habitable for humans and other species.

A lot of these things have to do with the way we live our everyday lives, especially the ways in which we consume, use, waste, and throw away things of value. Some of the categories in which we can improve our respectfulness of the environment are buying and consuming food carefully; using and not abusing energy in our homes and businesses and in our transportation choices; and recycling, reusing, and repurposing the goods that we no longer use.

For example, many of us who live in developed countries buy vehicles that are bigger than we need and that are "gas-guzzlers." Fortunately, we have an increasing ability to purchase more energy-efficient transportation such as fuel-efficient, hybrid, and electric vehicles. (One of the authors drives a Chevy Volt that gets the equivalent of over 80 miles of gasoline to the gallon. The other has a Toyota Prius that averages over 40 miles to the gallon, and an all-electric Nissan Leaf that doesn't use any gas at all.)

Even more energy-efficient than these options are biking and walking from home to work and other destinations. Also, depending on where we live, public transportation is a cheap and low-energy way to get from place to place.

Energy efficiency in homes and other buildings can have a huge impact on the consumption of electricity and natural gas. By combining more than one energy-efficiency technique (for example using LED light bulbs and appliances rated for their low-energy use) a household can reduce its energy usage and expenses by half.[133]

And, some of us can use renewable energy rather than fossil-fuel-based energy for heating and cooling our homes and other buildings, and for charging our plug-in vehicles. (One of the authors had solar panels installed on his home before he moved into an apartment. With a fairly small solar array, he reduced the cost of his annual electricity consumption by $600.) There is also a growing phenomenon called community-based solar power, in which solar arrays are constructed to serve a community or neighborhood.

There are about 1 billion people, mostly living in developing countries, who do not have access to electricity. A decentralized network of solar mini-grids could serve many of these people at a relatively low cost and without spewing carbon dioxide into the atmosphere.[134] The rapidly decreasing cost of solar and wind energy, and battery-storage systems, have made these energy sources as reliable as fossil-fuel options and at costs competitive with fossil-fuel options, including natural gas.[135]

2. Limit species extinction

Climate change is a key factor threatening the survival of thousands of plant and animal species. Thus, to the extent that we are successful in limiting the increase in the earth's surface temperature, we will also reduce the rate of species extinction.

However, as we saw in Chapter 7, greenhouse-gas emissions are one of many causes of species extinction. Others include habitat loss and degradation, overexploitation (hunting, harvesting, poaching, etc.), invasive species, and pollution.

We humans are responsible for most of these other factors that are threatening so many of the earth's species. An important takeaway from the diverse causes of species extinction is that addressing problems of climate change alone does not solve the extinction problem.

For example, we continue to destroy forests, especially in tropical areas, that are home to hundreds of thousands of plant and animal species. According to FAO (the United Nations Food and Agricultural Organization) we destroyed 129 million hectares of forests between 1990 and 2015. A piece of good news is that we have cut in half the deforestation rate during this time period.[136] (One hectare is equal to 2.5 acres or 10,000 square meters.)

We should keep in mind that creating a more sustainable environment will require changes in human behavior on many levels, and that many of the negative ways in which we are impacting the planet are related to one another. Reducing deforestation and increasing good forest management have multiple benefits, including a reduction in the rate of species extinction and the reduction of carbon dioxide going into the atmosphere.

Ultimately, we need to change the way we interact with our natural surroundings. Too often, we treat air, water, land, plants, and animals as things to exploit and misuse. If we are ever to attain a more cooperative society, we need to recognize that we are part of nature, and that if we abuse it, the consequences come back to disrupt our lives, as the problems of global warming clearly illustrate.

Concluding comments on recommendations and observations

We have presented recommendations consistent with the theme that we, as humans, shape the world in which we live. We do this as individuals and small groups, geographical communities, other groups of people working together, countries, groups of countries, and as a world society, such as through the United Nations. We can act strategically at each of these levels to improve our performance on a range of activities that can move us closer to becoming a cooperative society.

Section D:
Conclusion

Conclusion

We have presented the hypothesis that human beings may be on the verge of a new stage of history, which we refer to as the cooperative society. After elaborating on the stages of history to date and what this new stage might look like, we analyzed seven broad economic, political, social, and environmental measures to determine whether they are tending toward or away from a transition to the cooperative society. We made a series of observations and recommendations that either build on progress toward a cooperative transition or counter current trends away from such a transition.

Our main conclusion is that at this point in human history, there are divergent trends, some moving toward increased cooperation and others undermining it. On the plus side, cooperative businesses appear to be growing in number and global influence; the number of deaths from conflict around the world has dropped sharply since the end of World War II; the number of democracies and people living in democracies has risen dramatically since the beginning of the 20th century; and the quality of life in both developed and developing countries has shown significant improvement in the last 25 years.

On the negative side, a relatively small number of for-profit corporations dominate the global economy; income and wealth are inordinately concentrated in the hands of a very small percentage of the world's population; and the most ominous environmental indicator, the temperature of the earth's surface, has risen to its highest level in 125,000 years due primarily to human-generated emissions of greenhouse gases.[137] We will see over the next several decades whether or not we can shift toward zero population growth before the end of the century.

The jury is still out on whether or not we are transitioning to the cooperative society. However, as we have stated throughout the book, we are not merely passive observers of these trends and countertrends. As humans, we can shape our own history.

That is the ultimate message of this book. We as a species are not destined to destroy ourselves and our planet. We can make the transition from a destructive society to a cooperative one. And we can make major progress on that transition between now and 2030.

Section E:
Appendices

Cooperative business opportunities

Following are a series of questions that should be explored in order to identify co-op opportunities over the next couple of decades.

What is the potential for co-op growth in the world's largest countries?

The global co-op census estimates that India has about 265 million co-op memberships, equivalent to approximately 20 percent of its population. There are 136 million co-op memberships in China, equivalent to about 10 percent of its population. The same data set shows only about 2 million co-op memberships in Indonesia, about 1 percent of its population.

What explains these differences? Are there co-op sectors in China and Indonesia (e.g., finance, insurance, farming, and/or others) that are ripe for rapid expansion? If so, how best can these opportunities be realized? China is the largest country in the world and has one of the fastest-growing economies. Indonesia is the fourth-largest country and its economy also is growing at a fairly rapid pace. Significant growth of the cooperative movement in these two countries would translate into hundreds of millions of new co-op memberships.

Systematic analysis of the potential for cooperative growth should be done for other countries and regions of the world as well, not just those with the largest populations.

What economic sectors have high potential for co-op and mutual growth?

As mentioned above, it appears that both financial co-ops and insurance co-ops and mutuals have been growing rapidly and have good potential to continue to do so.

Almost 90 percent of the world's 570 million farms are located in low- and middle-income countries. Agricultural supply, marketing, and service co-ops have a long history of success in developed countries and in some developing countries, such as India and Kenya.

Many examples over the past few years have shown the ability of co-ops to help farmers transition from subsistence and subsistence-plus farming to small-scale commercial farming. Tens of millions of farmers could become new members of co-ops in the next 12 years. What is the potential for increasing the number of agricultural co-ops and co-op members in developing countries during this time? How should it be accomplished?

How can the role of employee-owned cooperatives and multi-stakeholder co-ops (owned by multiple categories of members) be expanded over the next 12 years?

In a few countries, such as Spain, Italy, and France, employee-owned cooperatives are a significant part of the co-op movement, but on a world scale, they account for a very small percentage of co-ops and co-op memberships. Co-ops with multiple membership categories are present in quite a few countries, but, as with worker co-ops, represent a small minority of co-ops.

At the same time, there is tremendous potential for growth in these two co-op categories. For example, about 15 million employees in the United States work for companies that have employee stock ownership plans (ESOPs) or similar plans. This gives them ownership shares in their companies, but limited voting rights. A change in ESOP legislation could open the door for these employees to become voting shareholders, and in some cases to restructure their companies as co-ops.

In many sectors of the co-op economy, including services, retail, and agriculture, the opening up of membership to various combinations of consumers, employees, and producers has the potential to increase co-op memberships and also increase the number of co-ops. Home-care services is just one example of a co-op model in which providers and consumers could have joint decision-making power.

How should co-ops be involved in implementing the Paris Climate Change Agreement and the UN Sustainable Development Goals?

Here are just a few of the ways:

- **Agricultural and forestry co-ops** can be a means to mobilize rural people to adapt farm practices to droughts and other changes in weather patterns resulting from climate change, and to reduce carbon going into the atmosphere.

- **Energy co-ops,** especially those providing solar and other renewable services, can meet the increasing needs of urban and rural communities for affordable energy, and, at the same time, reduce reliance on fossil fuels and wood energy.

- **Community-based health cooperatives** can play an important front-line role in meeting important sustainable development goals, such as reducing child and maternal mortality and addressing AIDS-related problems, including providing access to anti-retroviral drugs, condoms, and education.

These are just a few examples of cooperatives related to energy, climate change, and health. If implemented on a large scale, they could create or expand tens of thousands of co-ops, and tens of millions of co-op memberships by 2030.

Selected readings

Dave Grace and Associates, "Measuring the Size and Scope of the Cooperative Economy: Results of the 2014 Global Census on Cooperatives," prepared for the United Nations Secretariat, Department of Economic and Social Affairs, Division for Social Policy and Development, www.un.org/esa/socdev/documents/2014/coopsegm/grace.pdf

Goldstein, Joshua S. and Steven Pinker, "The Decline of War and Violence," *The Boston Globe,* April 15, 2016, http://www.bostonglobe.com/opinion/2016/04/15/the-decline-war-and-violence/lxhtEplvppt0Bz9kPphzkL/story.html?event=event25

Harari, Yuval Noah, *Sapiens: A Brief History of Humankind,* HarperCollins Publishers, 2011.

International Co-operative Alliance, "Blueprint for a Cooperative Decade," 2013. ica.coop/sites/default/files/media_items/ICA%20Blueprint%20-%20Final%20-%20Feb%2013%20EN.pdf

International Co-operative Alliance and Euricse, "Exploring the Co-operative Economy: Report 2015." monitor.coop/sites/default/files/WCM_2015%20WEB.pdf

Milanovic, Branko, *Global Inequality: A New Approach for the Age of Globalization,* Belknap Press, 2016.

Piketty, Thomas, *Capital in the Twenty-First Century*, Belknap Press, 2014.

Pinker, Steven, *The Better Angels of Our Nature: Why Violence Has Declined*, Penguin Group, 2012.

Pinker, Steven, *Enlightenment Now: The Case for Reason, Science, Humanism, and Progress*, Penguin Books Limited/ Viking, 2018.

UNFCCC, "Report of the Conference of the Parties on its twenty-first session, held in Paris from 30 November to 13 December 2015." (Adoption of the Paris Agreement on Climate Change.) unfccc.int/resource/docs/2015/cop21/eng/10a01.pdf

United Nations General Assembly. "Transforming our world: The 2030 Agenda for Sustainable Development." October 21, 2015. www.un.org/ga/search/view_doc.asp?symbol=A/RES/70/1&Lang=E

The authors

E.G. Nadeau has a Ph.D. in sociology and has spent most of his more-than 45-year career developing, researching, writing, and teaching about cooperatives and community development in the United States and in developing countries.

Luc Nadeau has a Masters of Science degree in ecology and is an active environmentalist and artist. He prepared most of the visuals for this book.

Endnotes

Some links may have changed since this book was published.

1. Many scientists put the age of Homo sapiens at about 200,000 years. For example: Howell, Elizabeth, "How long have humans been on earth?" *Universe Today*, January 19, 2015. http://www.universetoday.com/38125/how-long-have-humans-been-on-earth/ Williams, Shawna, "Human Species May Be Much Older Than Previously Thought," *The Scientist*, September 29, 2017 https://www.the-scientist.com/news-opinion/human-species-may-be-much-older-than-previously-thought-30819

2. Many archeologists agree that the world's first cities were founded in Mesopotamia between 4,000 and 6,000 years ago. For example: Mark, Anthony J., "The Ancient City: Definition." *The Ancient History Encyclopedia*, April 5, 2014. http://www.ancient.eu/city/ We hypothesize that early cities marked a shift to a more highly stratified society than small agricultural-based villages.

3. For example, as articulated in "The Universal Declaration of Human Rights," United Nations, 1948. http://www.un.org/en/universal-declaration-human-rights/

4. Lee, Richard B. and Daly, Richard Heywood, *The Cambridge Encyclopedia of Hunters and Gatherers*. Cambridge University Press, Inside front cover, 1999.

5.   Pauls, Elizabeth Prine, "Hunting and gathering culture," *Encyclopaedia Britannica*, March 16, 2007. https://www.britannica.com/topic/hunting-and-gathering-culture See also: Howell, op. cit.

6.   For example: Gray, Alic William, "Origins of agriculture." *Encyclopaedia Britannica*, Last updated, September 29, 2015. https://www.britannica.com/topic/agriculture

7.   Mark, op. cit.

8.   Excerpt from the 2015 Introduction to the Universal Declaration of Human Rights, originally approved by the members of the United Nations in 1948. http://www.un.org/en/udhrbook/pdf/udhr_booklet_en_web.pdf

9.   Nash, Jay Robert, *Darkest Hours*, Rowman & Littlefield, 1976.

10.   Climate Change, United Nations, Accessed August 2018. http://www.un.org/en/sections/issues-depth/climate-change/

11.   Millennium Development Goals, United Nations Development Programme, Accessed August 2018. http://www.undp.org/content/undp/en/home/sdgoverview/mdg_goals.html

12.   Sustainable Development Knowledge Platform, United Nations, Accessed August 2018. https://sustainabledevelopment.un.org/?menu=1300

13.   Briggs, Helen, "What is in the Paris climate agreement?" By BBC News, May 31, 2017. https://www.bbc.com/news/science-environment-35073297

14.   Volcovici, Valerie, U.S. submits formal notice of withdrawal from Paris climate pact, August 4, 2017. https://www.reuters.com/article/us-un-climate-usa-paris/u-s-submits-formal-notice-of-withdrawal-from-paris-climate-pact-idUSKBN1AK2FM

15.   Sustainable Development Goal 13. Take urgent action to combat climate change and its impacts. https://sustainabledevelopment.un.org/sdg13

16.   United Nations Framework Convention on Climate Change, Accessed August 2018. https://www.iucn.org/theme/global-policy/our-work/united-nations-framework-convention-climate-change-unfccc

17. Shaer, Matthew, "The Archaeology of Wealth Inequality," *Smithsonian Magazine,* March 2018. https://www.smithsonianmag.com/history/aracheology-wealth-inequality-180968072/

18. Maverick, J.B., "The 4 Biggest Chinese Banks," Investopedia, August 2015. https://www.investopedia.com/articles/investing/082015/4-biggest-chinese-banks.asp

19. de la Merced, Michael J., "Saudi Aramco Public Listing May Be Delayed Until 2019," March 11, 2018. https://www.nytimes.com/2018/03/11/business/dealbook/saudi-aramco-public-listing-may-be-delayed-until-2019.html

20. "The World's Largest Public Companies, June 2018." *Forbes Global 2000,* https://www.forbes.com/global2000/list/#tab:overall

21. Wikipedia, "List of largest private non-governmental companies by revenue," April 2018. https://en.wikipedia.org/wiki/List_of_largest_private_non-governmental_companies_by_revenue

22. Ibid.

23. "What is Social Enterprise?" Social Enterprise Alliance, 2018. https://socialenterprise.us/about/social-enterprise/

24. Duda, John, "The Italian Region Where Co-ops Produce a Third of Its GDP," John Duda, July 5, 2016 http://www.yesmagazine.org/new-economy/the-italian-place-where-co-ops-drive-the-economy-and-most-people-are-members-20160705

25. Borzaga, Carlo and Galera, Giulia, "Social Enterprises and their Eco-systems: Developments in Europe, European Commission, Directorate-General for Employment, Social Affairs and Inclusion," 2016.

26. Ibid., p. 41.

27. Nadeau, E.G., "Businesses with a heart," January 2018. http://www.thecooperativesociety.org/2018/01/10/businesses-with-a-heart/

28. International Co-operative Alliance, http://ica.coop

29. Ibid.

30. Dave Grace and Associates, "Measuring the Size and Scope of the Cooperative Economy: Results of the 2014 Global Census on Co-operatives." For the United Nation's Secretariat, Department of Economic and Social Affairs, Division for Social Policy and Development, April 2014. http://www.un.org/esa/socdev/documents/2014/coopsegm/grace.pdf

31. Keep in mind a couple of things about these data: The results of the global census are adjusted to include mutual insurance policyholders. "Memberships" include some people who are members of more than one co-op or mutual. Therefore, an individual or organization may have more than one membership.

32. Dave Grace and Associates, op cit.

33. World Bank (2016), "Gross Domestic Product 2015," http://databank.worldbank.org/data/download/GDP.pdf

34. Euricse is an acronym for the European Research Institute on Cooperatives and Social Enterprises. http://www.euricse.eu

35. http://monitor.coop/en/media/resources?field_media_type_tid percent5B percent5D=7

36. "Exploring the Cooperative Economy," Report 2016. https://cooperativesforabetterworld.coop/material/2016-world-co-op-monitor/ Exploring the Cooperative Economy, Report 2017. https://cooperativesforabetterworld.coop/material/2017-world-co-op-monitor/

37. World Council of Credit Unions, http://www.woccu.org/about/intlcusystem

38. "The World's Biggest Public Companies," 2016 Rankings. *Forbes Global 2000*, http://www.forbes.com/global2000/

39. World Bank, "Listed Domestic Companies, 2015, Total," 2016. http://data.worldbank.org/indicator/CM.MKT.LDOM.NO

40. Authors' calculation based on *Forbes* and World Bank data, op. cit.

41. "The World's Largest Public Companies in 2015," *Forbes Global 2000*, https://www.forbes.com/sites/liyanchen/2015/05/06/the-worlds-largest-companies/#52a0d9362ce4 Global 2000: The World's Largest Public Companies in 2016 https://www.forbes.com/sites/steveschaefer/2016/05/25/the-worlds-largest-companies-2016/#4ac2917145a6 Global 2000: The World's Largest Public Companies in 2017 https://www.forbes.com/sites/corinnejurney/2017/05/24/the-worlds-largest-public-companies-2017/#38739e5d508d Global 2000: The World's Largest Public Companies in 2018. https://www.forbes.com/global2000/#667ac0d335d8

42. "The World's Largest Public Companies in 2018," *Forbes Global 2000*, https://www.forbes.com/global2000/#667ac0d335d8

43. Elliott, Larry, "Inequality gap widens as 42 people hold same wealth as 3.7 billion poorest." *The Guardian*, January 21, 2018.

44. Credit Suisse, "Global Wealth Report 2015," p.18. https://publications.credit-suisse.com/tasks/render/file/?fileID=F2425415-DCA7-80B8-EAD989AF9341D47E

45. Kroll, Luisa, "Forbes Billionaires 2018: Meet The Richest People On The Planet," *Forbes,* March 6, 2018 https://www.forbes.com/sites/luisakroll/2018/03/06/forbes-billionaires-2018-meet-the-richest-people-on-the-planet/#4ea2529a6523

46. "Reward Work, Not Wealth," Oxfam, January 2018, p.2. https://d1tn3vj7xz9fdh.cloudfront.net/s3fs-public/file_attachments/bp-reward-work-not-wealth-220118-en.pdf

47. See for example: *The Economist* magazine's Crony Capitalism Index: https://www.economist.com/blogs/graphicdetail/2016/05/daily-chart-2. See also Jacobs, Didier, "Extreme Wealth is Not Merited," Oxfam, 2015. https://www.oxfam.org/sites/www.oxfam.org/files/file_attachments/dp-extreme-wealth-is-not-merited-241115-en.pdf

48. Milanovic, Branko, *Global Inequality*. Belknap Press, p.31, 2016

49. World Inequality Report, Executive Summary, 2018, pps. 7-9. https://wir2018.wid.world/files/download/wir2018-summary-english.pdf

50. "Reward Work," op.cit., p. 22.

51. Online Etymology Dictionary. https://www.etymonline.com/word/conflict

52. "Research Starters: Worldwide Deaths in World War II," National World War II Museum, New Orleans, Accessed August 22, 2018. https://www.nationalww2museum.org/students-teachers/student-resources/research-starters/research-starters-worldwide-deaths-world-war

53. Pinker, Steven, *The Better Angels of Our Nature.* Belknap Press, 2012.

54. Pinker, Steven, "Has the Decline of Violence Reversed since *The Better Angels of Our Nature* was Written?" 2014. http://stevenpinker.com/files/pinker/files/has_the_decline_of_violence_reversed_since_the_better_angels_of_our_nature_was_written.pdf

55. Ibid.

56. Pinker, 2012, op. cit.

57. Roser, Max, "War and Peace," 2018. https://ourworldindata.org/war-and-peace

58. "Global Violent Deaths, Small Arms Survey," December 2017. P. 20. http://www.smallarmssurvey.org/fileadmin/docs/U-Reports/SAS-Report-GVD2017.pdf

59. Croucher, Shane, "Civilian Deaths Surge Amid Wars in Syria and Yemen," *Newsweek*, April 4, 2018. https://www.newsweek.com/civilian-deaths-surge-amid-wars-syria-and-yemen-883417

60. Ibid.

61. Roser, op. cit.

62. "Global Violent Deaths," op. cit.

63. Merriam-Webster, https://www.merriam-webster.com/dictionary/democracy

64. The Polity Project, Center for Systemic Peace, 2017. http://www.systemicpeace.org/polityproject.html

65. "Democracy Index 2017, Free Speech Under Attack," The Economist Intelligence Unit. http://www.eiu.com/topic/democracy-index

66. Marshall, Monty G. and Cole, Benjamin R., Global Report 2014: "Conflict, Governance and State Fragility." Center for Systemic Peace. http://www.systemicpeace.org/globalreport.html

67. Authors' calculation.

68. "Democracy Index 2015: Democracy in an age of anxiety." The Economist Intelligence Unit (2016). http://www.eiu.com/public/topical_report.aspx?campaignid=DemocracyIndex2015

69. The Polity Project, 2017, op. cit.

70. The Economist Intelligence Unit, 2017, op. cit.

71. World Population Clock. http://www.worldometers.info/world-population/

72. "World population projected to reach 9.8 billion in 2050, and 11.2 billion in 2100," United Nations Department of Economic and Social Affairs, June 21, 2017. https://www.un.org/development/desa/en/news/population/world-population-prospects-2017.html

73. Malthus, T. R., "An Essay on the Principle of Population," Oxford World's Classic Reprint, 1798.

74. Ehrlich, Paul R., *The Population Bomb*, Ballantine Books, 1968.

75. Cartalucci, Tony, "World Population Alarmism: Twelve Billion People by 2100," Centre for Research on Globalization, September 23, 2014. https://www.globalresearch.ca/world-population-alarmism-twelve-billion-people-by-2100/5403796

76. "Family planning/Contraception," World Health Organization, February 2018. http://www.who.int/news-room/fact-sheets/detail/family-planning-contraception

77. "The Accuracy of Past Projections, Chapter 4 in Beyond Six Billion: Forecasting the World's Population." National Research Council. 2000. Washington, DC: The National Academies Press. https://www.nap.edu/read/9828/chapter/4

78. Roser Max, "Fertility Rate," Our World in Data, 2017. https://ourworldindata.org/fertility-rate

79. "Guttmacher-Lancet Commission Proposes a Bold, New Agenda for Sexual and Reproductive Health and Rights," May 9, 2018. https://www.guttmacher.org/news-release/2018/guttmacher-lancet-commission-proposes-bold-new-agenda-sexual-and-reproductive

80. "Extreme Poverty," Nuru International, undated. http://www.nuruinternational.org/why/extreme-poverty/

81. "Goal 1: No poverty," United Nations Development Program, 2018. http://www.undp.org/content/undp/en/home/sustainable-development-goals/goal-1-no-poverty.html

82. Collins Dictionary. https://www.collinsdictionary.com/us/dictionary/english/quality-of-life

83. United Nations Development Programme, Human Development Report 2015. http://hdr.undp.org/sites/default/files/2015_human_development_report.pdf.

84. United Nations, The Millennium Development Goals Report 2015.http://www.un.org/millenniumgoals/2015_MDG_Report/pdf/MDG%202015%20rev%20(July%201).pdf

85. United Nations Development Programme, Human Development Report 2016. http://hdr.undp.org/sites/default/files/2016_human_development_report.pdf

86. De Vos, Jurriaan, M.; Joppa, Lucas N.; Gittleman, John L.; Stephens, Patrick R.; and Pimm, Stuart L., "Estimating the normal background rate of species extinction." *Conservation Biology*. Volume 29, Issue 2, pages 452–462, April 2015.

87. "The Big Five Mass Extinctions," *Cosmos*. https://cosmosmagazine.com/palaeontology/big-five-extinctions.

88. "Dinosaur Extinction," *National Geographic*, undated. https://www.nationalgeographic.com/science/prehistoric-world/dinosaur-extinction/

89. Living Planet Report 2016, World Wildlife Federation. https://www.worldwildlife.org/pages/living-planet-report-2016

90. "IUCN Red List of Endangered Species," International Union for Conservation of Nature, 2015. https://www.iucn.org/theme/species/our-work/iucn-red-list-threatened-species

91. Some of the reported increase in threatened species presented in the graph may be a result of better measurement rather than increased threat of extinction. That is, we know more about the number and types of plants and animals in the world in 2018 than we did in 1996. As a result, some of the reported increase in threatened species may reflect our improved knowledge rather than more species under threat. However, this is likely to be a minor factor in the rapidly increasing trend reported in the data.

92. "Global Temperature," NASA, 2015. http://climate.nasa.gov/vital-signs/global-temperature/.

93. World Wildlife Foundation, op. cit.

94. Global Climate Report – Annual 2017, National Centers for Environmental Information. https://www.ncdc.noaa.gov/sotc/global/201713

95. Malala Yousafzai, Wikipedia, Accessed July 2018. https://en.wikipedia.org/wiki/Malala_Yousafzai

96. Keneally, Meghan, "How gun laws have changed in 4 states since the Parkland shooting," ABC News, March 22, 2018. https://abcnews.go.com/US/states-gun-laws-changed-parkland/story?id=53902445

97. Harvey Weinstein sexual abuse allegations, Wikipedia. https://en.wikipedia.org/wiki/Harvey_Weinstein_sexual_abuse_allegations

98. Me Too Movement. https://metoomvmt.org

99. Bautista, Nidia, "What does Harvey Weinstein's arrest mean for the #MeToo movement?" Aljazeera, June 2018. https://www.aljazeera.com/indepth/features/harvey-weinstein-arrest-metoo-movement-180607141309271.html

100. Co-opLaw, an eResource Library. http://www.co-oplaw.org/co-op-basics/types/

101. COPAC, "Statistics on Cooperatives: COPAC takes action with expert workshop," 2016. http://www.copac.coop/statistics-on-cooperatives-copac-takes-action-with-expert-workshop/

102. International Co-operative Alliance, "Co-operative identity, values & principles," 2016. https://ica.coop/en/whats-co-op/co-operative-identity-values-principles.

103. Ibid, "1st International Forum on Co-operative Law," 2016. http://ica.coop/en/events/1st-international-forum-co-operative-law

104. Ibid, "Blueprint for a Co-operative Decade," 2013. https://www.ica.coop//sites/default/files/media_items/ICA%20Blueprint%20-%20Final%20version%20issued%207%20Feb%2013.pdf

105. There are approximately 25 organizations in Canada, Europe, and the United States that provide co-op development assistance in developing countries. For the most part, their work takes the form of project-by-project assistance to specific groups of co-ops over three- to five-year time periods. Much of this assistance is very useful, but it does not directly address the need for cooperative development support available in-country on a long-term basis. This lack represents a glaring shortcoming of this approach. (Comment based on one of the author's unpublished research projects.)

106. Bessen, James, "Lobbyists are behind the rise in corporate profits." *Harvard Business Review*, May 26, 2016. https://hbr.org/2016/05/lobbyists-are-behind-the-rise-in-corporate-profits

107. Nadeau, E.G., *The Cooperative Solution*. Self-published. pp. 31-33, 2013

108. Federal Trade Commission, "Merger review," 2016. https://www.ftc.gov/enforcement/merger-review

109. Mian, Atif and, Sufi, Amir, *House of Debt*, University of Chicago, 2014

110. O'Brien, Matt, "The miraculous story of Iceland." *Washington Post*, June 17, 2015. https://www.washingtonpost.com/news/wonk/wp/2015/06/17/the-miraculous-story-of-iceland/

111. Michon, Kathleen, J.D., "Tobacco Litigation: History & Recent Developments." Nolo, 2015. https://www.nolo.com/legal-encyclopedia/tobacco-litigation-history-and-development-32202.html

112. Golshan, Tara, "Ruth Bader Ginsburg says her 'impossible dream' is for Citizens United to be overturned." Vox, updated, July 11, 2016. www.vox.com/2016/7/11/12148066/ruth-bader-ginsburg-citizens-united

113. Luhby, Tami, "'Scandinavian Dream' is true fix for America's income inequality." CNN Money, June 3, 2015. http://money.cnn.com/2015/06/03/news/economy/stiglitz-income-inequality/

114. Piketty, Thomas, *Capital in the Twenty-First Century*, Belknap Press, 2014.

115. Luhby, op. cit.

116. "10 Principles of Fair Trade," World Fair Trade Organization, November 2017. https://wfto.com/fair-trade/10-principles-fair-trade

117. Center for Global Development, "Commitment to Development Index 2017." https://www.cgdev.org/sites/default/files/commitment-development-index-2017.pdf

118. Grinshteyn, E., and Hemenway, D., "Violent Death Rates: The US Compared with Other High-income OECD Countries," 2010, *American Journal of Medicine*, March 2016. https://www.ncbi.nlm.nih.gov/pubmed/26551975

119. "The Assault Weapon Myth," *New York Times*, September 14, 2014. https://www.nytimes.com/2014/09/14/sunday-review/the-assault-weapon-myth.html

120. Charbonneau, Louis and Nebehay, Stephanie, "Iran, world powers reach initial deal on reining in Tehran's nuclear program." Reuters, April 2, 2015. http://www.reuters.com/article/us-iran-nuclear-idUSKBN0MQ0HH20150402.

121. Gurney, C., "A Great Cause: The Origins of the Anti-Apartheid Movement", *Journal of Southern African Studies*, Vol. 26, No. 1, pp. 123–144, 2000.

122. "Human Rights and Democracy," European Union, January 2018. http://www.europarl.europa.eu/RegData/etudes/PERI/2017/600413/IPOL_PERI(2017)600413_EN.pdf

123. Anti-apartheid movement, Wikipedia. https://en.wikipedia.org/wiki/Anti-Apartheid_Movement

124. Babones, Salvatore, "A Rural Incubator for China's Political Reform?" *Foreign Affairs*, October 14, 2015. https://ses.library.usyd.edu.au/bitstream/2123/16641/2/Country%20lessons.pdf

125. "Sexual and Reproductive Health: Overcoming barriers to adolescent health education and services," World Health Organization, undated. http://www.who.int/reproductivehealth/topics/adolescence/education/en/

126. "Family planning/Contraception," World Health Organization, February 2018. http://www.who.int/news-room/fact-sheets/detail/family-planning-contraception

127. "Sustainable Development Goals: 17 Goals to Transform Our World," undated. http://www.un.org/sustainabledevelopment/sustainable-development-goals/

128. "The definition of extreme poverty has just changed," Overseas Development Institute, October 5, 2015. https://www.odi.org/comment/9934-extreme-poverty-definition-world-bank-sustainable-development-goals

129. Sustainable Development Goals, op. cit.

130. Adoption of the Paris Agreement, United Nations Climate Change. https://unfccc.int/resource/docs/2015/cop21/eng/l09r01.pdf

131. Ibid.

132. "America is still in. Are you?" https://www.wearestillin.com

133. "How Much Can You REALLY Save with Energy Efficient Improvements?," Energy.gov offices.Ohttps://www.energy.gov/energysaver/articles/how-much-can-you-really-save-energy-efficient-improvements

134. "Mlinda – Solar mini-grids for off-grid rural markets (India)," Alliance for Rural Electrification, undated. https://www.ruralelec.org/project-case-studies/mlinda-solar-mini-grids-grid-rural-markets-india

135. "Clean energy is catching up to natural gas. The natural gas 'bridge' to sustainability may be shorter than expected," Roberts, David, Vox, August 8, 2018. https://www.vox.com/energy-and-environment/2018/7/13/17551878/natural-gas-markets-renewable-energy

136. "World deforestation slows down as more forests are better managed," FAO, September 2015. http://www.fao.org/news/story/en/item/326911/icode/

137. "Earth's last major warm period was as hot as today," Sumner, Thomas, Science News, January 19, 2017. https://www.sciencenews.org/article/earth's-last-major-warm-period-was-hot-today

138. Cooperative and mutual insurance members/policyholders (millions). Source: The International Cooperative and Mutual Insurance Federation.

139. Battle deaths from 1946-2015. Uppsala Conflict Data Program (UCDP) & Peace Research Institute Oslo (PRIO). https://ourworldindata.org/war-and-peace

140. Historical and projected fertility rates. Source: UN "World Population Prospects: The 2017 Revision."

CPSIA information can be obtained
at www.ICGtesting.com
Printed in the USA
FFHW01n0439191018
48842157-53044FF
Printed thr IngramSpark
50-lb-paper